Classics in Psychology
1855–1914

A Collection of Key Works

Thoemmes / Maruzen

Classics in Psychology, 1855–1914

A Collection of Key Works

Edited by **Robert H. Wozniak,** *Bryn Mawr College*

Robert H. Wozniak, *Guide to Classics in Psychology, 1855–1914* (1999)

1. A. Bain, *The Senses and the Intellect* (1855)
2. H. Spencer, *The Principles of Psychology* (1855)
3. A. Bain, *The Emotions and the Will* (1859)

4/5. G. T. Fechner, *Elemente der Psychophysik* (1860)

6. F. Galton, *Hereditary Genius* (1869)
7. H. Maudsley, *Body and Mind* (1870)
8. H. Taine, *On Intelligence* [1870] (1871)
9. H. L. F. Helmholtz, *On the Sensations of Tone* [3rd ed., 1870] (1875)
10. W. Wundt, *Grundzüge der physiologischen Psychologie* (1874)
11. W. B. Carpenter, *Principles of Mental Physiology* (1874)
12. F. Galton, *English Men of Science* (1874)
13. D. Ferrier, *The Functions of the Brain* (1876)
14. G. H. Lewes, *The Physical Basis of Mind* (1877)
15. T. Ribot, *German Psychology of To-Day* [1879] (1886)
16. R. H. Lotze, *Outlines of Psychology* [1881] (1886)
17. J. H. Jackson, *Evolution and Dissolution of the Nervous System* [orig. pts, 1881–7] (1932)
18. H. Höffding, *Outlines of Psychology* [1882] (1891)
19. F. Galton, *Inquiries into Human Faculty and Its Development* (1883)
20. H. Ebbinghaus, *Memory* [1885] (1913)
21. H. Bernheim, *Suggestive Therapeutics* [1886] (1889)
22. A. Binet, *The Psychology of Reasoning* [1886] (1899)
23. E. Mach, *Contributions to the Analysis of the Sensations* [1886] (1897)
24. G. T. Ladd, *Elements of Physiological Psychology* (1887)
25. G. J. Romanes, *Mental Evolution in Man* (1888)
26. C. L. Tuckey, *Psycho-Therapeutics* (1889)

27/28. W. James, *The Principles of Psychology* (1890)

29. W. Wundt, *Lectures on Human and Animal Psychology* [2nd ed., 1892] (1894)
30. P. Janet, *The Mental State of Hystericals* [1892–4] (1901)
31. O. Külpe, *Outlines of Psychology* [1893] (1895)
32. J. M. Baldwin, *Mental Development in the Child and the Race* (1895)
33. C. L. Morgan, *Habit and Instinct* (1896)
34. E. B. Titchener, *An Outline of Psychology* (1896)
35. W. Wundt, *Outlines of Psychology* [1896] (1897)
36. J. M. Baldwin, *Social and Ethical Interpretations in Mental Development* (1897)
37. L. T. Hobhouse, *Mind in Evolution* (1901)
38. E. L. Thorndike, *An Introduction to the Theory of Mental and Social Measurements* (1904)
39. M. Prince, *The Dissociation of a Personality* (1906)
40. O. Pfungst, *Clever Hans (The Horse of Mr. Von Osten)* [1907] (1911)
41. A. Forel, *The Senses of Insects* (1908)
42. E. B. Huey, *The Psychology and Pedagogy of Reading* (1908)
43. W. McDougall, *An Introduction to Social Psychology* (1908)
44. W. D. Scott, *The Psychology of Advertising* (1908)
45. M. F. Washburn, *The Animal Mind* (1908)
46. R. Schulze, *Experimental Psychology and Pedagogy* [1909] (1912)
47. E. Claparède, *Experimental Pedagogy and the Psychology of the Child* [1910] (1911)
48. E. L. Thorndike, *Animal Intelligence* (1911)
49. H. Münsterberg, *Psychology and Industrial Efficiency* (1913)
50. E. L. Thorndike, *Educational Psychology* (1914)

Dates in square brackets indicate the original French or German editions from which these first English translations were prepared.

The Psychology of Advertising

A Simple Exposition of the Principles of Psychology in their Relation to Successful Advertising

WALTER DILL SCOTT

THOEMMES PRESS

MARUZEN CO., LTD

This edition co-published in 1998 by

THOEMMES PRESS
11 Great George Street
Bristol BS1 5RR, United Kingdom

MARUZEN CO., LTD
3–10, Nihombashi, 2-chome, Chuo-ku
Tokyo, 103–8245 Japan

The Psychology of Advertising
ISBN 1 85506 694 7

Classics in Psychology, 1855–1914
50 volumes : ISBN 1 85506 602 5

British Library Cataloguing-in-Publication Data
A CIP record of this title is available from the British Library

Printed in England by Antony Rowe Ltd, Chippenham

Publisher's Note

The Publisher has gone to great lengths to ensure the quality of this reprint but points out that some imperfections in the original book may be apparent.

This book is printed on acid-free paper, sewn, and cased in a durable buckram cloth.

THE PSYCHOLOGY OF ADVERTISING

A Simple Exposition of
The Principles of Psychology
In Their Relation to
Successful Advertising

By WALTER DILL SCOTT, *Ph.D.*

Director of the Psychological Laboratory of Northwestern University

Boston
Small, Maynard & Company
1908

CONTENTS

LIST OF ILLUSTRATIONS

LIST OF ILLUSTRATIONS

THE PSYCHOLOGY OF ADVERTISING

I
INTRODUCTION

THE typical business man is an optimist. For him the future is full of possibilities that never have been realized in the past. He is not, however, a day-dreamer, but one who uses his imagination in formulating purposes which lead to immediate action. His power of execution often surpasses that of his imagination, and he is frequently surprised to see his vision realized in less time than he had even dared to hope.

The advertiser may well be regarded as typical of the class of American business men. At a time when advertisements were poorly constructed and given limited circulation, certain enterprising men saw the possibilities of advertising and began systematically to improve the whole profession of advertising. Artists were employed to construct appropriate illustrations, and skilled typographers vied with each other in setting up the text in the most artistic and legible manner possible. Business system was used in ascertaining the amount of circulation of various publications as well as the kind of circulation. Advertisements were keyed, and other means were employed to discover the exact value of each style of advertisements and of each medium in which advertisements were inserted.

These improvements have been as beneficial as the most sanguine could have hoped for, but in and of themselves they were not sufficient to place advertising upon a scientific basis. Advertising has as its one function the influencing of human minds. Unless it does this it is useless and destructive to the firms attempting it. As it is the human mind that advertising is dealing with, its only scientific basis is psychology, which is simply a systematic study of those same minds which the advertiser is seeking to influence. This fact was seen by wise advertisers and such conceptions began to appear in print and to be heard in conventions of advertising men some ten years ago. Occasionally one who was especially optimistic prophesied that at some time — perhaps in the distant future — advertisers would turn to psychology for guidance. One such prophecy appeared in *Printers' Ink* for October, 1895: "Probably, when we are a little more enlightened, the advertisement writer, like the teacher, will study psychology. For, however diverse their occupation may at first sight appear, the advertising writer and the teacher have one great object in common — to influence the human mind."

Printers' Ink seemed to assume that it would be many years before we were "more enlightened," and hence did not look to see advertisers actually turning to psychology in the immediate future. In *Publicity,* for March, 1901, we have a more hopeful prophet, and although each expects to see advertising established on psychological principles, the author in *Publicity* hopes to see that day in the near future: "The time is not far away when the advertising writer will find the inestimable value of a knowledge of psychology."

Previous to the appearance of this article (March, 1901) there had been no attempt to present psychology to the business world in a usable form. As far as the advertiser could see all psychologies were written with a purely theoretical end in view. They contained a vast amount of technical material devoid of interest to the layman who struggled through the pages. This condition made it quite difficult for the business man to extract that part of the subject which was of value to him.

Several of the leading advertising magazines and advertising agencies sought to father a movement which would result in such a presentation of the subject of psychology that it would be of use to the intelligent and practical advertiser. These efforts on the part of the advertisers were successful in stimulating several professional psychologists to attempt such a presentation. Psychological laboratories were fitted up to make various tests upon advertisements. Elaborate investigations were undertaken and carried through to a successful issue. Psychologists turned to the study of advertising in all its phases while, on the other hand, intelligent and successful advertisers began to devote attention to a systematic study of psychology. Investigators in the various parts of the country and among different classes of society united in their efforts to solve some of the knotty problems which are ever before the business man who desires publicity for his commodity. Soon addresses were made before advertising clubs upon the specific topic of the psychology of advertising. The leading advertising journals in America and Europe sought and published articles on the subject. Several of the recent books on advertising and general business promotion deal more or less extensively with the subject.

As a result of all these various efforts more has actually been accomplished during the last five years than the typical optimist even imagined. Just as the manufacturing world has been compelled to turn its attention to physics and chemistry, and as the manufacturer's vocabulary is composed of many terms which were but recently technical terms used only by scientists, so the advertising world has turned its attention to the subject of psychology, and many words formerly used only by professional psychologists are to-day commonplaces with advertisers.

The changed attitude of the advertising world can be judged by reference to current advertising literature. In a recent issue of *Printers' Ink* (July 24, 1907), one article has this significant heading, "PSYCHOLOGICAL." Another article by a leading advertiser contains the following sentences. "Scientific advertising follows the laws of psychology. The successful advertiser, either personally or through his advertising department, *must* carefully study psychology. He *must* understand how the human mind acts. He *must* know what repels and what attracts. He *must* know what will create an interest and what will fall flat. . . . He *must* be a student of human nature, and he *must* know the laws of the human mind." Although italics were not used in the original, the word "must" is here put in italics to draw attention to the actual emphasis used by the author. In articles appearing on the subject before the last few years, all persons had spoken of the study of psychology as something which might be brought about in the future. At the present time the writers are asserting that the successful advertiser *must* study psychology and that he *must* do it at once.

Although the attitude of the advertising world has changed and even though much has been done to present psychology in a helpful form to the advertisers, the work of the psychologist is not yet available to the business world because the material has not been presented in any one accessible place. Contributions are scattered through the files of a score of American and European publications. Some articles appearing under this head are of minor significance, while others are so important that they should be collected in a place and form such that they would be available to the largest possible number of readers. The psychology of advertising has reached a stage in its development where all that has thus far been accomplished should be reconsidered. The worthless should be discarded and the valuable brought out into due prominence in systematic arrangement. In view of this condition of affairs the author has assumed the pleasing task of systematizing the subject of the psychology of advertising and of presenting it in such a form that it will be of distinct practical value to all who are interested in business promotion.

Incidentally it is hoped that the present volume will be welcomed by many who have no especial interest in business promotion. The professional psychologist will be interested in the contribution made to his science from a study of mind in a particular field of activity. The general reader will derive benefit from the reading of the book; for he will be able to grasp some of the most fundamental psychological principles because they are here presented in concrete and comprehensible form.

II
MEMORY

IMPRESSIONS once received leave traces of themselves, so that, in imagination, we can live over the same experiences and can recognize them as related to our past. This knowledge of former impressions, or states of mind, which have already once dropped from consciousness, is what is known as memory.

I can imagine how the jungles of Africa must look. This is an act of productive imagination. Yesterday I was on the corner of Fifth avenue and Lake street in Chicago. I heard the shouts of teamsters, the rattle of passing vehicles, and the roar of elevated trains; I saw the people, the wagons, and the cars. To-day I can, in imagination, live over the same experience, and as I do so I recognize the experience as belonging to my past. I am therefore remembering my past experience.

As I try to recall the street scene of yesterday I find that many of the details have escaped me. I cannot remember how the teamsters looked nor what sort of cries they were uttering. I remember that there were teamsters and that they were shouting at their horses, but I cannot, in my imagination, see their faces or hear their voices as I did yesterday. In short, my memory has faded, and has faded rapidly. It is not likely that any memory is so vivid as the original experience, neither does it contain all the details of the actual experience. Immediately after crossing the street I could have described the scene much better than I could now. A year hence I shall probably have forgotten all about it.

Our memories gradually fade with time. Professor Ebbinghouse, of Germany, was the first to try to find out exactly how fast our memories do fade. Since he published his thesis many others have taken up the work, and his and their results are fairly well established and definite. They have found that our memories are at their best two seconds after the experience has taken place. After two seconds the memory fades very rapidly, so that in twenty minutes we have forgotten more of an experience than we shall forget in the next thirty days.

We forget very rapidly during the first few seconds, minutes and hours. What we remember a day is a very small part of our experiences, but it is the part which persists, as the memory fades very slowly after the first day. What we remember for twenty minutes and what we can get others to remember for that time is of great concern, for it is what we and they remember for longer times also.

What the practical business man wants to know about memory can be put in two questions.

First, how can I improve my own memory?

Second, how can I so present my advertisements that they will be remembered by the public?

It is not possible for a person with a poor memory

to develop a good one, but every one can improve his memory by the observance of a few well-known and thoroughly established principles. The first principle is *repetition.* If you want to make sure that you will remember a name, say it over to yourself. Repeat it in all the ways possible — say it over aloud, write it, look at it after it is written, think how it sounded when you heard the name, recall it at frequent periods and until it has become thoroughly fixed in your mind.

Four Principles of Improving One's Own Memory

The second principle is *intensity.* If you want to remember a name, pay the strictest possible attention to it. If you apply the first principle and repeat the name, then you should pay the maximum amount of attention to every repetition. In this way the process of learning will be so reduced that a single repetition may be enough, and still the name may be retained for a long period of time.

The third principle is that of *association.* The things which we think over, classify and systematize, and thus get associated with our previous experience, are the things which we commit most easily and retain the longest.

As a boy at school I learned by repetition that Columbus discovered America in 1492. At that time this was to me an entirely disconnected fact. It was not associated with anything else, and so cost me great effort of attention and frequent repetition before I had it thoroughly memorized. At a later time I was compelled to learn the approximate date of the fall of Constantinople, the application of the compass to navigation, the invention of printing, the time of the activity of Copernicus, Michelangelo, Titian, Dürer, Holbein, etc. Such a list of unconnected dates would have cost me much unprofitable effort if I had been compelled to learn them separately. As it was, I connected them all with the date of the discovery of America, and saw that these men and these events were all contemporaneous and together made what is known as the Renaissance.

The details of a business or professional life which are connected in a series are not hard to learn, and are not soon forgotten. A man may have no trouble from forgetting the details of his business or profession, yet may have a poor memory for all events not thus associated.

The fourth principle is that of *ingenuity*. I remember the name of Miss Low, for she is a short woman. I remember a friend's telephone, which is 1391, by thinking how unfortunate it is to have such a number to remember—13 is supposed to be an unlucky number, and 91 is seven times 13.

This method is applicable only to disconnected facts which we find difficulty in remembering by the methods given before. It is, however, a method which was used by the Roman orators and has been used more or less ever since. There is probably no one who does not make frequent use of it in attempting to remember names, dates, figures and similar data.

We all appreciate the value of a good memory, and are willing to pay any one who will tell us how to train ours. This condition of affairs has made "memory training" a profitable business for the fakir. It is fairly well established now that one's native retentiveness is unchangeable. One who has an unretentive memory cannot possibly change it by any method of training. All he can do is to improve on his method of acquiring and recording knowledge.

The third principle given above — association — is the one by far of the most importance.

The fourth principle is the one of least general application; indeed if an attempt is made to apply it too frequently, it becomes worse than useless, yet it is the principle used by most persons who have "memory training" to sell.

Which Advertisements are Remembered?

When the question arises,— how to construct an advertisement so that the reader cannot forget it, we find that the question is answered by the proper application of the principles enunciated above. The advertisement that is repeated over and over again at frequent intervals gradually becomes fixed in the memory of the reader. It may be a crude and an expensive method, but it seems to be effective.

This method gains added effect by repeating one or more characteristic features, and by changing some of the features at each appearance of the advertisement. Thus the reproduced advertisement of Vitalized Phosphites (No. 1) is frequently repeated in identical form. We cannot forget this advertisement,

VITALIZED PHOSPHITES.

Brain and Nerve Food,

From the phosphoid principle of the Ox Brain and the Embryo of Wheat.

Has been used more than thirty years by thousands of active business men and women, from whom sustained, vigorous application of brain and nervous power is required, promptly relieving the depression from overwork, worry, nervous excitement, and sleeplessness, increasing activity and vital force by feeding the brain and nerves with the exact food they require for their nutrition and normal action.

May we send you a descriptive pamphlet?

PREPARED BY

56 West 25th Street, New York City.

If not found at Druggist's, sent by mail ($1.00).
CROSBY'S COLD AND CATARRH CURE.
The best remedy in existence for cold in the head and sore throat. By mail, 50 cents.

No. 1.— This advertisement is engraved on the memory by the expensive process of mere repetition.

but it has taken too many repetitions to secure the desired results.

The reproduced advertisement of Cream of Wheat (No. 2) is but one of a series of advertisements in all of which the colored chef appears prominently. This characteristic feature causes us to associate all of the series, and hence the effect of repetition is secured. At the same time, there is sufficient diversity, because the colored chef is never represented in the same way in any two of the advertisements as they appear from month to month. Similar statements could be made of a host of other excellent advertisements.

No. 2.— This series of advertisements represents the central feature, but always in a new form.

The Second Principle Applied

The advertisement which makes an intense impression is one which the advertiser does not easily forget. The methods for securing this intensity are many, but a few examples will serve to make the method plain.

Bright colors impress us more than dull ones. The bright-colored inserts and advertisements run in colors are remembered better than others, because they make a greater impression on us.

In any experience it is the first and the last parts of it that impress us most and that get fixed most firmly in our memories. The first and the last advertisements in a magazine are the most effective. Likewise the first and the last parts of any particular advertisement (unless very short) are the parts that we remember best.

The back cover-page is valuable because when the magazine is lying on a table the back cover-page is likely to be turned up, but in addition to that it is a valuable page because it is likely to be the first or the last seen by most readers.

The second cover-page is valuable because it is so likely to be seen first, and even to be seen by those who do not look at the advertisements in the back of the magazine—if such persons still exist!

The intensity of the impression which an advertisement makes is dependent upon the response which it secures from the readers. The pedagogue would call this action the "motor response," even though it were nothing more than the writing of a postal card. Such action is vital in assisting the memory of the readers.

An advertisement which secures a response sufficient to lead to the writing of a postal card has a chance of being remembered which is incomparably greater than that of other advertisements. The advertisement of Pompeian Massage Cream (No. 3) will not soon be forgotten by those who are induced

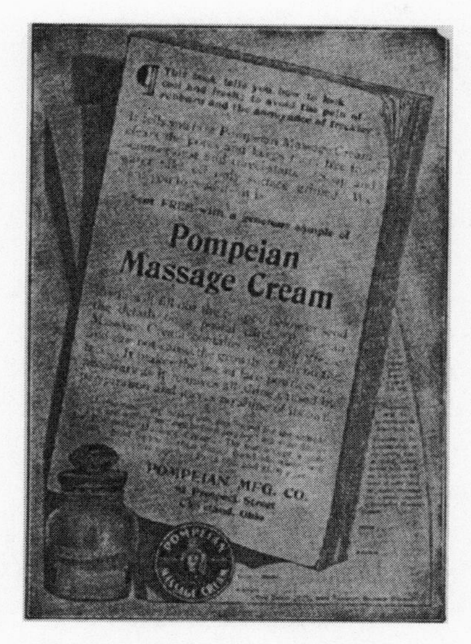

No. 3.— Those who answer this advertisement will not easily forget it.

to send the name of their dealer to the Pompeian Manufacturing Company.

Rhymes and alliterations are rhetorical forms which seem to be of great assistance when we attempt to commit verses, and even when we do not want to remember them the rhythm may make such an impression that we can't forget them. The " Spotless

Town " is an illustration of a successful application of this psychological fact.

There is much poor advertising being done at the present time in a futile attempt to produce a successful imitation of the " Spotless Town." The rhythm and the alliteration must be excellent, else they make

No. 4.—Those who laugh at this advertisement will remember it.

the whole attempt seem ridiculous, and the advertisement falls flat.

Anything humorous or ridiculous — even a pun — is hard to forget. But unless the attempt is successful, the result is ludicrous and futile. Furthermore, that which impresses one person as funny may seem silly to another. The reproduced advertisement of Gold Dust (No. 4) seems funny to some, but does not to others. The reproduced advertisement of

Rough on Rats (No. 5) impresses some persons as silly, while others think it funny.

Advertising is a serious business, and unless the advertisement is extremely clever, it is unwise to attempt to present the humorous side of life, although it is highly valuable when well done.

Anything will be remembered which awakens our emotions, whether the thing be ugly or beautiful,

No. 5.— An evident attempt to be humorous.

whether it causes us to smile or to sympathize with the sorrows of others. That which excites an emotion is not easily forgotten, and hence is a good form of advertising, if it can convince the reason at the same time that it stimulates the feelings. The advertisement of Gold Dust (No. 4) pleases me and convinces me that the product is good. The advertisement of Rough on Rats (No. 5) amuses me because it is so excessively silly. It does not please me, does not convince me of the desirability of the goods. I find that both advertisements have made such an intense impression on me that they have stuck in my memory. and I see no prospect of being able to forget them soon.

The writer of advertisements must consider the principle of association, and ordinarily does so, even if he does it unconsciously. He should present his argument in such a form that it will naturally and easily be associated by the reader with his own former experience. This is best done by appealing to those interests and motives which are the ruling principles of the reader's thinking. Personally, I should forget a recipe for a cake before I had finished reading it, but to a cook it is full of interest, and does not stand out as an isolated fact, but as a modification or addition of something already in his mind. The statement that the bond bears four per cent. interest is not forgotten by the capitalist; for he immediately associates the bond of which this statement is made with the group of similar bonds, and so the statement is remembered, not as an isolated fact, but in connection with a whole series of facts which are constantly before his mind.

The Third Principle Applied

The arguments of an advertisement should be such as are easily associated with the personal interests and with the former experience of the majority of the readers.

The reproduced advertisement of the Buster Brown Stocking Co. (No. 6) is in direct violation of this principle. The advertisement was evidently written by a man, and appeals to men as being a good advertisement. It would be remembered by men, and if they were the purchasers of boys' stockings, it would be an

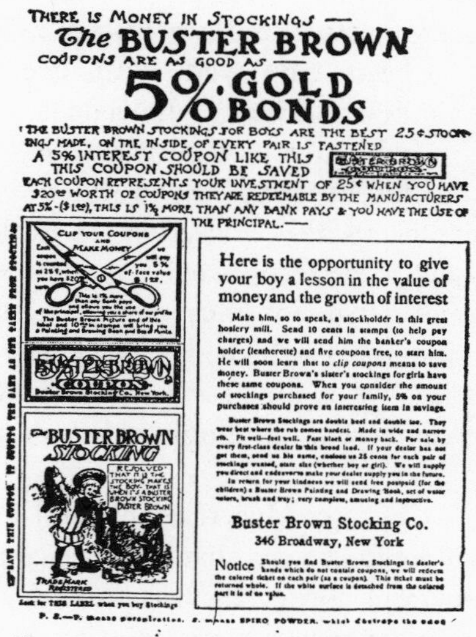

No. 6.— The wrong associations suggested.

excellent advertisement. In reality the men do not buy the stockings, and so the advertisement appeals to those who have nothing to do with the business — except those who pay for the advertisement.

The following expressions appeal powerfully to a manufacturer, but not to a mother:

"Five per cent. gold bonds," "Clip your coupons and make money," "Give your boy a lesson in the value of money and the growth of interest," "This is one per cent. more than any bank pays, and allows you the use of the principal, allowing you a share of our profits," etc.

The principle of ingenuity can have but an occasional application, but there are instances when it has been employed with great effectiveness. Thus "Uneeda" is a name which cannot be forgotten. It pleases by its very ingenuity, although most of the attempts in this direction have been futile. Thus "Uwanta" is recognized as an imitation, and is neither impressive nor pleasing. "Keen Kutter" is a name for tools which is not easily forgotten. "Syrup of Figs" is a name for a patent medicine which is easily remembered, although the product contains no figs.

The Fourth Principle Applied

A tailor in Chicago advertised himself and his shop in such an ingenious way that no one could read his advertisement and forget the essential features of it. His street number was 33, his telephone number was the same. There were 33 letters in his name and address. He sold a business suit for $33. The number 33 stood out prominently as the striking feature of his advertisement and impressed many as being unique, and at the same time fixed in their minds his name and address, and the cost of his suits.

The four principles enunciated above for impressing advertisements on the minds of possible customers are capable of unlimited application, and will not disappoint any; for they are the laws which have been found to govern the minds of all persons as far as their memories are concerned.

III
THE FEELINGS AND THE EMOTIONS

We all know what is meant by pleasure and pain, by joy and grief. These feelings and emotions are not better understood after we have attempted to define them. They are known only by experience, and we are all familiar with them. In the present chapter we are interested in the effect which pleasure and pain and the different emotions have upon the mind and the body of the person experiencing them. These effects are not sufficiently recognized and yet they are of special significance to the advertiser.

For the sake of brevity we shall use the word pleasure not merely to express such simple pleasures as tasting an appetizing morsel, but also to express such pleasurable emotions as joy, love, benevolence, gratitude, pride, etc. The word pain or displeasure will likewise be used to express simple painful sensations and also emotions which involve pain, such as fear, hate, jealousy, antipathy, etc.

Effects of Pleasure and Pain

Every pleasurable and every painful experience has a direct reflex effect on the bodily functions and also on the action of the mind. These effects are widespread and important. Some of these changes, even though significant, are not directly detected without the use of delicate recording instruments.

Pleasures actually cause the limbs to increase in size, and, accompanying the physical change, is a feeling of expansiveness which serves to heighten the pleasure. With pain the limbs shrivel in size, and this is accompanied by a feeling of depression.

Under the influence of pleasure the efficiency of the heart-action is greatly enhanced. This increase of blood supply gives us a feeling of buoyancy and increased vitality, which greatly enhances the already pleasing experience. Displeasure, on the other hand, interferes with the normal action of the heart. This gives us a feeling of sluggishness and depression.

Pleasure assists the rhythmical action of the lungs and adds to the depth of breathing. These changes serve but to add to the already pleasing experience. Pain interferes with the rhythm of breathing, makes the lung action less deep, and gives a feeling of being stifled, hindered and checked in carrying out our purposes.

Pleasing experiences increase our muscular strength and cause us to feel like men. We feel more like undertaking great tasks and have more faith in our ability to accomplish them. Pain decreases muscular strength and gives us a feeling of weakness and lack of confidence.

Pleasures not only give greater strength to the voluntary muscles, but they affect directly the action of all the voluntary and involuntary muscles of the body. In pleasure the hands go out from the body, the shoulders are thrown back and the head elevated. We open up and become subject to the influences in our environment. Being pleased with what we are receiving, we become receptive and expand that we may take in more of the same sort. In pain the hands are drawn in towards the chest and the whole body draws in within itself as if to protect itself against outside influences. These actions of the body are reflected in the mental attitude. In pleasure our minds expand. We become extremely suggestible, and are likely to see everything in a favorable light. We are prompt to act and confident of success. In pain we are displeased with the present experiences and so withdraw within ourselves to keep from being acted upon. We refuse to receive suggestions, are not easily influenced, and are in a suspicious attitude toward everything which is proposed. When in pain we question the motives of even our friends and only suspicious thoughts are called up in our minds.

These brief statements of facts serve to call to the reader's attention the mental attitude in which the person is placed by the influence of pleasure and pain. Keen observers of men have not been slow in profiting by these facts. In "*Pickwick Papers,*" speaking from the view-point of the defendant, Dickens says: "A good, contented, well-breakfasted juryman is a capital thing to get hold of. Discontented or hungry jurymen always find for the plaintiff." Here Dickens

Appealing to Customers Through Their Feelings

expresses the fact that man is not pre-eminently logical, but that his thinking is influenced by his present state of feelings. If the juryman were discontented and hungry, he would be feeling pessimistic and suspicious and would believe in the guilt of the defendant.

The modern business man does his utmost to minister to the pleasure of the customers in his store. He knows that they will place a larger order if they are feeling happy than if they are feeling otherwise. The American slang expression, "jolly up," means the pleasing by flattery of the one from whom it is desired to obtain a favor. The merchant attempts to please the customer by the appearance of the store, by courteous treatment and by every other possible method. The same pains must be taken by the advertiser in his attempts to please those to whom his appeals are made. The methods open to the advertiser are relatively few and hence all available means should be employed most assiduously.

In the present chapter the importance of pleasing the advertiser by appealing to his esthetic sense will be emphasized, and suggestions will be given of concrete methods which are available to the advertiser in appealing to the sense of the beautiful.

To be beautiful a thing must possess certain characteristics which awaken a feeling of appreciation in the normal person. It is true that the artistic judgment is not possessed equally by all, or at least it is not equally developed in all. There are, however, certain combinations of sounds which are universally called harmonies and others which are called discords. There are certain combinations of colors which are regarded as pleasing and others which are displeasing. There are likewise certain geometrical forms or space arrangements which are beautiful, and others which are displeasing. The musician knows what tones will harmonize and which ones will not. The man without a musical education does not possess such knowledge, but he appreciates the harmony of tones when he hears it. The colorist knows how to produce pleasing effects with colors. He has acquired this knowledge which others do not possess, although they are able to appreciate his work. The artist knows how to produce pleasing effects with symmetry and proportion of space forms. The uninitiated does not possess such knowledge or ability, although he is able to appreciate the work of the artist and can distinguish it from the work of the novice.

Beauty Appreciated Though Not Understood

Perhaps the simplest thing that could be suggested which would have an element of esthetic feeling connected with it is the bisection of a straight line. It seems almost absurd to suppose that the position of the point of division in a straight line would have anything to do with a feeling of pleasure. Such, however, is certainly the case, but, as might be expected, the esthetic feeling is not very pronounced. As an illustration, look at No. 1. Here we have a series of straight lines divided by short cross lines. Look at the lines carefully and you will probably feel that the lines A, B and C are divided in a more pleasing manner than F, G and H. In other words, if a straight vertical line is to be divided into two unequal parts, you prefer to have the division come above the

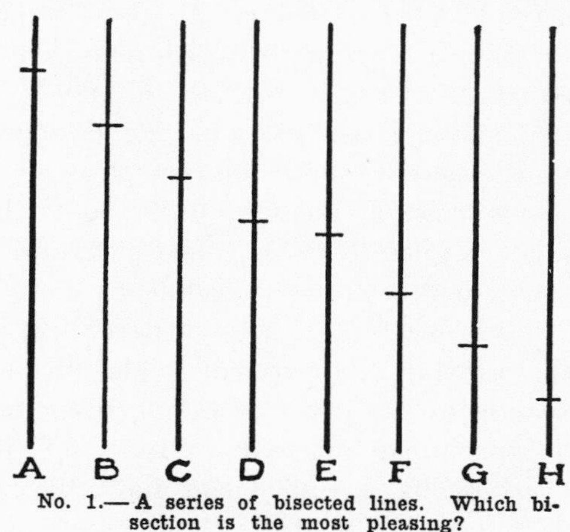

No. 1.—A series of bisected lines. Which bisection is the most pleasing?

middle. This is not an altogether unimportant discovery.

In judging of vertical distances, we over-estimate the upper half. For this reason the line E, which is divided into two equal parts, appears to be divided into two slightly unequal parts and the lower section seems to be the smaller. The line D is divided at a point slightly above the middle, but it appears to be divided into two exactly equal parts. Many persons would say that the line D is more pleasing than E, for D appears to be divided into two equal parts, while E appears as if an unsuccessful attempt had been made to divide the line into two equal parts.

Line D seems to be perfectly symmetrical—its two parts appear equal. The symmetry about this division pleases us, and most persons would say that this line, which is divided symmetrically, is more pleasing than A or H, which are not divided symmetrically.

The two parts of the lines A, B, C and H appear too unequal and the two parts of line E appear too nearly equal. Lines C and F are very pleasing. They have divisions which do not seem to be too much alike, so the divisions give diversity. The parts are not so different that they destroy the feeling of unity in the line. A line is pleasing if its two parts are not too much alike and not too different. The ratio of the smaller section of the line to the larger section in C and F is approximately that of 3 to 5. That is to say, if a vertical line is eight inches long, the result is pleasing if the line is divided into two sections which are respectively 3 and 5 inches long. Exact experimentation and measurements of artistic productions show that there is a remarkable preference for this ratio, which is known as the "golden section." The exact ratio is that of 1 to 1.618, which is approximately that of 3 to 5. A line is divided most artistically, if the lower section is 1.618 times as great as the upper. Although this fraction seems very formidable, it is the arithmetical expression of a simple proportion which is this: the short section is to the longer section as the longer section is to the sum of both sections. Any division of a line which approximates this golden section is pleasing, but a division which approximates the symmetrical division (and is not quite symmetrical) is displeasing.

If you hold No, 1 sideways, the lines will all be changed from vertical to horizontal. The divisions will now assume a new relation. The divisions of lines A, B and C cease to be more pleasing than those of F, G and H. E now seems to be divided symmetrically and is more pleasing than D. In fact, for most persons the symmetrical divisions of E seem to be more pleasing than those of even C and F, which are divided according to the ratio of the "golden section." The most pleasing division of a horizontal line is that of perfect symmetry and the next most pleasing is that of the "golden section."

In these divisions of straight lines into two equal parts unity is secured; in the divisions according to the ratio of the golden section diversity is secured, and the unity is not entirely lost. Unity and diversity are essential elements in all esthetic pleasures. In vertical lines we seem to prefer the emphasis on the diversity, while in horizontal lines the exact symmetry, or unity, is most pleasing.

Artistic Divisions of Forms

The discovery of the most pleasing proportion between the parts of straight lines would be of decidedly more importance if we should find that the same ratio holds for the parts of more complicated figures. Is a rectangle more pleasing than a square? (For the sake of brevity of expression we disregard the fact that a square is a particular form of a rectangle.) Men have been called on to decide this question times without number. By investigating a very large number of such decisions we may be able to discover something of value. The architect is called upon to decide this question every time he constructs a building in which the artistic effect plays any part — and it always should. Think of the temples, palaces, cathedrals, cottages, museums and all other structures in which the artistic element plays a large part. In a great proportion of these the height is not equal to the width. The individual rooms not infrequently bear the same ratios as the height and width of the entire building. Careful measurement of such structures has revealed a striking tendency to approximate what we have learned as the "golden section." In fact, it was originally called the "golden section of architecture," because it was discovered so uniformly in architecture.

Think of the shape of the flags of all nations, of all the picture frames which you have ever seen, of window panes, mirrors, playing cards, sheets of paper, envelopes, books, periodicals and all other objects in which the shape is determined to a greater or less extent by artistic demands. In most of these objects we find a very decided tendency to make the height equal the width, or else the height is to the width approximately as 3 is to 5.

Look at the square and the rectangle in No. 2. The height of the rectangle is to its base as 3 to 5. Most persons say that the rectangle is the more pleasing; some have a preference for the square. In the square we have a very decided symmetry. Each line is equal to every other line. A straight line drawn through the center of the figure from any angle divides the figure into two equivalent parts. In the rectangle the height is not equal to the length, but a line drawn through

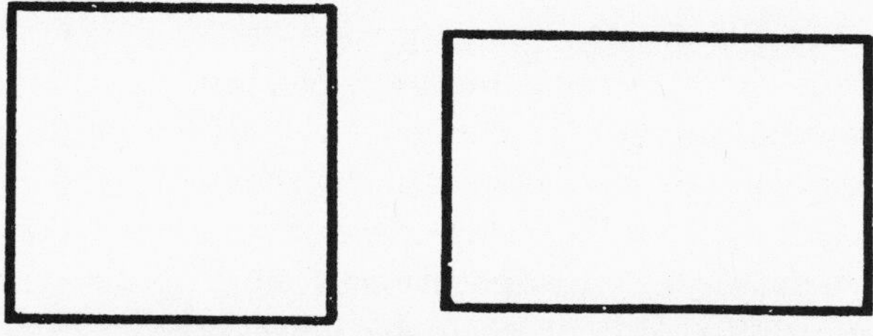

No. 2.— A square and a rectangle. Which is the more beautiful?

the center of the figure divides it into two equivalent parts. The square seems to possess much symmetry but little diversity. The rectangle possesses both unity and diversity.

A very careful investigator of the esthetic value of the different space forms gives some interesting results as the fruits of his labors. Thus, a rectangle whose base is three per cent. greater than the height is more pleasing than the perfect square. This is accounted for because we overestimate the height of a square about three per cent. Thus the rectangle whose base is three per cent. greater than its height appears to be a perfect square and so is more pleasing than the perfect square. If the height of a rectangle is approximately eighteen per cent. greater or less than its base, the figure is displeasing because it looks like an imperfect square. If the difference in the two dimensions of the rectangle becomes as great as forty per cent., the effect is pleasing because the difference is great enough to make it evident that the figure was not meant for a square. If one dimension of the rectangle exceeds the other approximately sixty per cent., we have the ratio of the "golden section," and the result is more pleasing than it is for any other ratio of base to height. If one dimension of a rectangle exceeds the other by more than two hundred and fifty per cent., the result is not satisfactory. The difference between the two dimensions seems to become too great and the unity of the figure is weakened.

When we consider that the ratio of one dimension to the other is but a minor element in the total esthetic effect, we are not surprised that we find exceptions to the conclusions reached in the foregoing, but the surprising thing is the lack of more exceptions. Buildings that exceed in height the ratio as given here do not look beautiful, and if the disproportion becomes great because of the excessive height, we call the buildings skyscrapers and regard them as eyesores to the American cities. A building whose width is many times its height is usually ugly and is designated as a shed.

That which has been said of the square and the rectangle holds equally true for the circle and the ellipse. A circle is a pleasing form which pleases because of its symmetry and regularity. An ellipse that is too much like a circle is much less pleasing than an ellipse in which the smaller diameter is to the greater one as 3 is to 5. The same holds true of a triangle also.

Artistic Form for Advertisements

The space used by an advertiser is usually a rectangle. In choosing this space, does the advertiser take into consideration the relation of the height and width which will produce the most pleasing effect? He certainly does and the space he chooses meets the conditions of esthetic pleasure as given above, although he may be entirely unconscious of any such intention. Thus in an ordinary magazine the full page and the ordinary quarter-page (the upper right, upper left, lower right and lower left) approximates most nearly the "golden section."

Next in the approximation to the standard is the division into upper and lower halves; next comes the horizontal quarter, and last the division into right and left halves. This order of esthetic effect is also the order of frequency of choice of space. The fact that a right or left half-page may be next to reading matter makes this division more popular than it otherwise would be. Turn over the pages of advertisements in any magazine and look at the different spaces to see which class of spaces pleases you most and which least, and you will probably choose the spaces in the order as indicated above. (No mention has been made of small advertisements, but what has been said of the larger spaces holds true of the smaller also.)

Some advertisers have used narrow spaces which extend entirely across the page. The effect has not been pleasing, although such shapes might be striking, because of their oddity. It is to be hoped that no publisher will allow the pages of his magazine to be chopped up into vertical quarters, for the effect would be most inartistic.

Artistic Subdivisions of Advertisements

The artistic subdivisions of spaces follow the laws of symmetry and proportion as given above. Almost every artistic production can be subdivided into two equivalent parts by drawing a vertical line through the middle of it. Such symmetry as this is called bilateral symmetry. As a typical example of bilateral symmetry as well as pleasing proportion in an advertisement we reproduce herewith the advertisement of the Butler Paper Company (No. 3). The line drawn vertically through this advertisement divides it into two symmetrical parts. Every subdivision of the display and of the text is centered. The horizontal divisions are strictly bilateral symmetry. Dotted lines are drawn to indicate the vertical divisions. In this we see that the subdivisions are not equal, but increase from the bottom upward in a pleasing proportion. A marked display is found in the words " Snow Flake," which serve to divide the text into two unequal divisions which are related to each other in a pleasing proportion. Such an arrangement of the vertical subdivisions is certainly more pleasing than equal subdivisions would be. By such subdivisions as we have here the unity of the page is not destroyed, and diversity is secured.

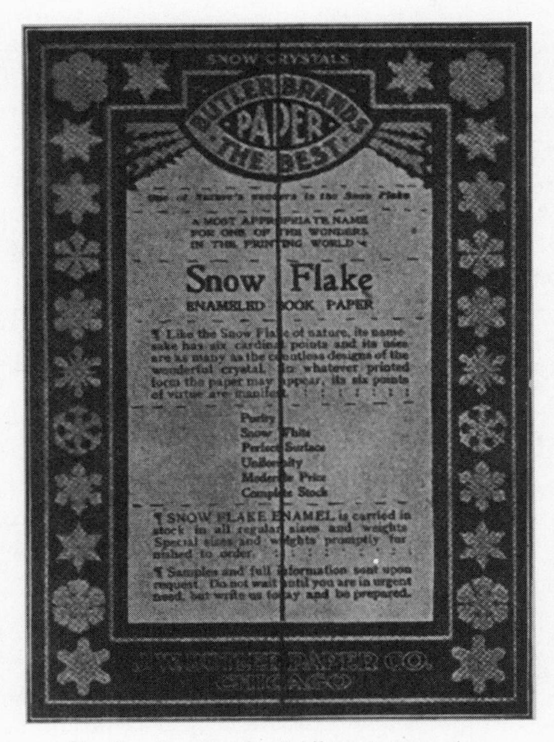

No. 3.— An example of bilateral symmetry.

It should be observed that this advertisement of the Butler Paper Company has employed an unusually large number of figures which are symmetrical and many more which are arranged on the ratio of the "golden section." As a result, pleasing unity and diversity are both secured. The symmetry is pronounced in the twenty-four crystals or stars which are used as a decoration in the border. There are twelve different kinds of stars, but each star has six main subdivisions and six minor subdivisions. There are enough stars to give diversity, and the stars are sufficiently alike to give unity to the border as a whole.

The white rectangle on which the text is found is slightly too long to be in the exact ratio of the golden section, while the darker border is too wide to meet the condition, but these rectangles are as near to the ratio of the golden section as could be produced in such a complicated figure as this.

It is no accident that the conventional ellipse at the top of the advertisement is in the same ratio as the rectangles, i. e., that of the golden section. If this advertisement were either lengthened or shortened, its proportions would vary from that of the "golden section," and the results would be recognized by the ordinary observer as less satisfactory.

It is not necessary to exaggerate the importance of these laws of symmetry and proportion. They contribute an appreciable amount to the beautification of the advertising page and hence to the production of pleasure in the mind of every possible customer who sees the advertisement. Inasmuch as the pleasure of the customer is of such fundamental importance the advertiser cannot afford to neglect any element which contributes to the total pleasurable effect. There are other laws which are of importance in giving a pleasing effect to a page. Among such laws might be mentioned ease of comprehension, ease of eye-movement, appropriate point of orientation and utility.

Space will not admit of a presentation of these principles but the purpose of this chapter has been attained if the reader has become impressed with the importance of pleasing the possible customer and with the significance of such simple laws as that of proportion and symmetry in accomplishing the desired result. These laws are of universal application in laying out advertisements and in choosing spaces, and an appreciation of their importance by the advertisers of the land would lead to a beautification of the advertising pages of our publications and hence to an increase in their value to the advertiser.

IV
APPEALS TO THE CUSTOMER'S SYMPATHY

In the last chapter we saw the significance of pleasure and pain in inducing the proper attitude in the minds of the customers. We also saw how a pleasing effect could be produced by the judicious use of the laws of symmetry and proportion in constructing advertisements. In the present chapter we shall continue the general discussion of the benefit of awakening the feelings and emotions and will confine the discussion to a single emotion, namely, that of sympathy.

By sympathy we mean in general a particular mental attitude which is induced by the realization of the fact that some one else is going through that particular form of experience. Thus I laugh and feel happy because those about me are rejoicing, and I weep because I see my friends weep. To a certain extent we seem to imagine ourselves as in the condition actually experienced by those about us and hence feel as we assume they must feel. The feelings awakened sympathetically are intense enough to cause weeping, laughing and all the ordinary forms of expressing the emotions.

We are not indifferent as to the objects upon which we bestow our sympathy. I feel no sympathy with the tree that is struck by the woodman's axe nor for the stone that is crushed under the wheels of a traction engine. I may feel sympathy for the mouse whose nest is destroyed or for the horse that is cruelly treated. I sympathize with animals because I believe that they have feelings similar to mine. I feel more sympathy for the higher animals (dogs and horses) than I do for the lower animals, for I believe that their feelings are more like mine. I have a certain amount of sympathy for all humanity, but I sympathize most with those of my own set or clique, with those who think the same thoughts that I think and who are in every way most like myself. After those of this inner circle of acquaintances, my sympathy is greatest for those whom I might call my *ideals*. If I desire to be prosperous, I feel keen sympathy with the man who appears to be prosperous. If I am ambitious to be a well-dressed man, I feel sympathetically towards those who are well dressed. If I desire to attain a certain station in life, I feel sympathetically with those who appear to have attained my ambition.

Sympathy for Our Ideal Selves

In the advertisement of Thomas Cook & Co. (No. 1) I do not think of the old lady and gentleman as being of my class. They are not my ideals and I therefore have comparatively little sympathy with them. They are enjoying themselves immensely and probably never had a better time in all their lives than they are having as members of this touring party, but as I look at them I am not pleased at all. Their

Illustrations From Advertisements

pleasure is not contagious so far as I am concerned. I seem to be immune from all their pleasures. I have

No. 1.— I do not share their pleasures.

no desire to imitate their actions and become a member of Cook's touring party.

In contrast with this Thomas Cook advertisement that of the Santa Fe Railroad (No. 2) may well be considered. The two persons here represented approximate my ideals. They seem to be enjoying the train immensely. I believe that they have good taste

No. 2.— They are enjoying the train.

and if they choose the California Limited for their wedding trip that train would certainly be desirable for my trips too. In every case of sympathy we imitate to a certain degree the objects of our sympathy. These passengers on the Santa Fe stimulate me to imitate their action, i. e., to get aboard the train and enjoy its luxuries.

No. 3.—Ridiculous but not ludicrous.

No. 3 is a reproduced advertisement of a fat-reducing compound. The illustration is supposed to be ludicrous, but to me it is ridiculous. The fat lady in the illustration does not seem to make the best of a bad situation. She dresses in plaids, which, as every corpulent person knows, serve but to increase the apparent size. Both the lady and the gentleman are the kind of people whom we do not admire, who are far from our ideals and who present but few elements of likeness to ourselves. The material advertised might be good for such persons as the illustration depicts, but that is no reason for me to imitate their actions and become one with them in any line of action.

No. 4 is a reproduction of an advertisement of a fat-reducing tablet, and the illustration is that of a lady who at once begets my sympathy. She is apparently making the best of a bad condition. If she is going to use the Howard Obesity Ointment, it certainly must be worth considering. I feel sorry for her and sympathize with her in her affliction. She certainly feels about the matter just as I should, and consequently it is easy for me to imagine myself in her stead and to feel the need for relief from obesity and to take the necessary steps to secure such relief.

The tragedy and the comedy are forms of literature and of dramatic representations which have always been popular. There is scarcely a tragedy without its comic parts, but frequently there are comedies without any element of the tragic. There are probably more great tragedies than comedies, but it is true that the ordinary men and women read more comedy (including the comic in a so-called tragedy) than tragedy, and that the same holds true for their attendance upon dramatic representations.

In a comedy the rollicking fun may be introduced immediately, and the reader or the spectator may be brought into the spirit of the whole at once without danger of any shock to the sensibilities because of the

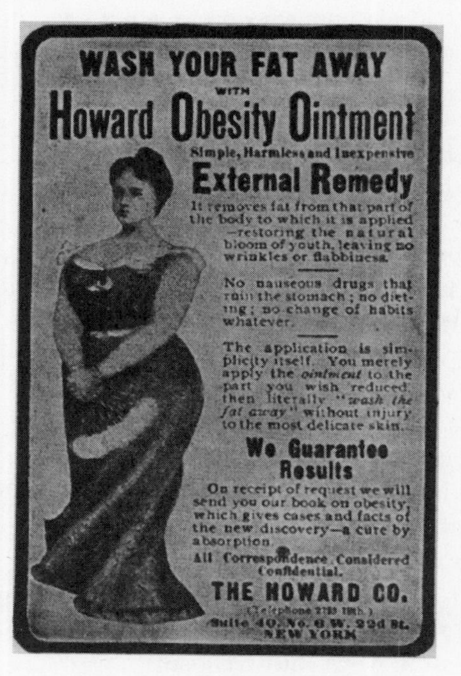

No. 4.— She begets my sympathy.

suddenness of the introduction of the emotional element.

In tragedy the reader or the spectator is usually introduced gradually into the emotional tone of the whole. The hero (if it be the hero who suffers) is first introduced, and then after we feel acquainted with him and have an interest in him, we are called upon to enter into his sorrows and to feel with him.

In a political campaign the politician may relate the instances of wrong and oppression for which the opposing party is responsible, or else he may tell of the prosperity and good cheer brought about by his own party. In raising money to found a charitable institution the philanthropist may tell of the squalor and misery of the persons in the district in which the institution is to be located, or else he may tell of the joys which the institution will bring into the lives of the persons concerned. In appealing for funds to carry on the missionary work in Africa the minister may describe the deplorable and almost hopeless condition of the natives, or else he may tell of the wonderful successes of the missionaries already on the field, and appeal for funds to continue the already successful work. It certainly is questionable which method the politician, the philanthropist, the minister, etc., should follow. As far as my personal observations go, it seems to me that when sympathy for sorrow is successfully awakened, it is more effective in bringing about the desired action than is sympathy for the joys of the persons concerned. It must be remembered, however, that the persons for whom the appeal is being made in all these cases are those for whom the hearers have more than a passing interest, and the creating of this interest may be the product of a long process of education. It may also be true that these most successful pathetic appeals would be avoided in the future by the very persons who had been moved most effectively. The depiction of the darker sides

No. 5.—An outrage upon the reader's sensibility.

of life may be very effective, but the depiction of the rosier hues is more attractive to most people.

It is said that savages laugh more loudly than persons in civilized countries, and in general loud or boisterous expressions of pleasure are not regarded as in good taste. Culture and good breeding have decreed that we shall not express our griefs in the sight or hearing of others. In fact, it is not in good form to express grief at all. We are not allowed to parade our sorrows before the gaze of the public. It seems to be assumed that everyone has sorrows enough of his own and therefore should not be called upon to share the sorrows of others. This attitude towards expressions of grief seems to be quite universal, and is taken so much as a matter of course that we feel offended when persons seek to awaken our sympathy by any form of external manifestation. Even in dramatic representations the expressions which accompany sorrow or pain are largely subordinated to apparent attempts to stifle such manifestations. We weep more readily with those who seem to have great cause for weeping, but restrain it, than for those who give way to their feelings. This attitude towards the manifestations of sorrow often causes us to be offended by manifestations of suffering. Thus in No. 5 there is an appeal made to our sympathy in such a rude manner that we feel angered with the advertiser, if not with the publisher, for allowing us to be insulted by such an audacious attack upon our sensibilities.

Appeals to Sympathy Attract Attention

One function of representations of feelings and emotions is to attract attention. Thus No. 6 is one of the most attractive advertisements in the current issue of our magazines. The smile is very contagious and the whole effect is so clear and so pleasing that I can scarcely turn the page without stopping to look at it.

As far as the attention value is concerned, equally good results may be secured by representations of sorrow. Thus in No. 7 sorrow is depicted in such a

No. 6.— A successful appeal to sympathy for pleasure.

way that it succeeds in attracting the attention of the most casual reader of advertisements.

Nos. 6 and 7 are reproductions of advertisements which represent the opposite sorts of feelings, and each awakens its appropriate kind of sympathy, and yet it is difficult to tell which advertisement has the greater attentive value. Personally, I enter into the

No. 7.—A successful appeal to sympathy for sorrow.

pleasure of the smiling young man more fully than I enter into the sorrow of the grief-stricken one.

These examples are sufficient to show that appeals

to the sympathy, either for pleasure or for pain, may be used with great profit by the advertiser. We are not cold, logical machines, but we are all human beings, with hearts in our breasts and blood in our veins, and we enjoy the depictions of real life with all its joys and sorrows. Whether the dark or the bright side of life offers the most material for the advertiser may be questionable, but there is certainly no question as to the advisability of appeals to the sympathies.

The time is coming, and indeed has come, when the advertising pages of our publications must be edited as carefully as the pages of the literary department. The advertising manager should not only refuse objectionable advertisers, but he should refuse all objectionable advertisements. It is quite possible that an advertisement which might be good for the individual advertiser would be injurious to the many who are occupying space in the same publication.

The advertisement reproduced in No. 5 may be good for the firm placing it. It may be attractive to such persons as need the cough syrup, but it may be so disgusting to all other persons that it renders them antagonistic and unsympathetic to all the advertisements seen for minutes after they have looked at this one. It might be a very profitable advertisement for Dr. Bull, but the advertising manager, by accepting it, has reduced the value of all other advertising spaces. The effect which would be produced on adjoining spaces by such advertisements as are shown in Nos. 1, 3 and 7 might also be questionable.

If you knew that one magazine carried advertisements which were pathetic in their illustrations and descriptions and that another magazine carried only bright and cheerful advertisements, which one would you pick up and look through? I believe that most persons would choose the magazine advertisements that present only the more cheerful aspects of life. If such is the case, it is the duty of advertising managers to see to it that the advertising pages of their publications are rendered attractive.

V
HUMAN INSTINCTS

We are all accustomed to think of the actions of animals as instinctive, but we are inclined to object to the application to human actions of anything which would obliterate the distinctions between human and animal actions, and we do not usually speak of the actions of man as being instinctive.

No one can carefully observe the actions of animals without being impressed with both the similarities and the differences between human and animal actions. In his native and ordinary environment the animal shows a cleverness of action which is hardly to be distinguished from that of a man. In a new environment and in the presence of unfamiliar objects, on the other hand, the animal displays a stupidity which is most astounding.

The animal has but few instincts, and these few are sufficient for his ordinary environment, but in the presence of environments unusual to his species he is at a loss as to his actions. Man possesses many more instincts than the animal and in addition has reason, which can control his instinctive actions and thus obliterate their instinctive appearance, although such actions are fundamentally instinctive.

An instinct is usually defined as the faculty of acting in such a way as to produce certain ends, without foresight of the ends, and without previous education in the performance. It is in this sense that the term is used throughout this discussion.

The following quotation from Professor James will undoubtedly prove of interest:

"*Now, why do the various animals do what seem to us such strange things,* in the presence of such outlandish stimuli? Why does the hen, for example, submit herself to the tedium of incubating such a fearfully uninteresting set of objects as a nestful of eggs, unless she has some sort of a prophetic inkling of the results? We can only interpret the instincts of brutes by what we know of instincts in ourselves. Why do men always lie down, when they can, on soft beds rather than on hard floors? Why do they sit around the stove on a cold day? Why do they prefer saddle of mutton and champagne to hard-tack and ditch-water? Why does the maiden interest the youth so that every thing about her seems more important and significant than anything else in the world? Nothing more can be said than that these are human ways, and that every creature *likes* its own ways, and takes to following them as a matter of course. Science may come and consider these ways, and find that most of them are useful. But it is not for the sake of their utility that they are followed but because at the moment of following them we feel that that is the only appropriate and natural thing to do. Not one man in a billion, when taking his dinner, ever thinks of utility. He eats because the food tastes good and makes him want more. If you ask him *why* he should want to eat more of what tastes like that, instead of revering you as a philosopher, he would probably laugh at you as a fool. The connection between the savory sensation and the act it awakens is for him absolute and needs no proof but its own evidence. It takes, in short, what Berkeley calls a mind debauched by learning to carry the process of making the natural seem strange, so far as to ask for the *why* of any instinctive human act. To the metaphysician alone can occur such questions as: Why do we smile, when pleased, and not scowl? Why are we unable to talk to a crowd as we talk to a single friend? Why does a particular maiden turn our wits so upside-down? The common man can only say, '*Of course* we smile, *of course* our heart palpitates at the sight of the crowd, *of course* we love the maiden, that beautiful soul clad in that perfect form, so palpably and flagrantly made from all eternity to be loved!'

"And so, probably, does each animal feel about the particular things it tends to do in the presence of particular objects. To the lion it is the lioness which is made to be loved; to the bear, the she-bear. To the broody hen the notion would probably seem monstrous that there should be a creature in the world to whom a nestful of eggs was not the utterly fascinating and precious and never-to-be-too-much-sat-upon object which it is to her.

"Thus we may be sure that, however mysterious some animals' instincts may appear to us, our instincts will appear no less mysterious to them. And we may conclude that, to the animal which obeys it, every impulse and every step of every instinct shines with its own sufficient light, and seems at the moment the only eternally right and proper thing to do. It is done for its own sake exclusively."

Every instinctive action is concrete and specific, and is the response of an individual directed toward some object. There is a great diversity in the methods of classifying instincts, and any method is justifiable if it is true and if it is helpful in making clear the nature of instincts, or is of service in any way. The classification we propose is justified in that it is true to the facts, and that it groups these actions in such a way that they may be better understood, and that the knowledge thus secured may be utilized.

As was said above, every instinctive action is directed toward some object, but the effect of the action is to bring the object into a relation which will make it helpful toward the preservation or furtherance of the interests of the individual or of the species. Thus when an animal acts according to his "hunting instinct" he acts toward his victim in such a way that he makes the victim serve his interests in providing food for himself and, perhaps, for others of his species. If instincts may be classified according as they tend toward the *preservation and furtherance of the interests of the individual,* our classification will be based upon the *interests* of the individual, which are preserved and furthered, rather than upon the manner of the preservation and furtherance.

The first interest of the individual which is instinctively preserved and furthered is his *material possessions.* The individual acts instinctively toward every material thing which he may call "*my*" or "*mine.*" Of all the material things to which I apply the term *my* or *mine,* there is nothing to which the term seems so applicable as to my *body.* This is so intimately mine that the distinction between it and *myself* or *me* cannot be definitely drawn. I avoid extremes of temperature, not because I think that thus I can preserve and further the development of the body, but because it is pleasant for me to act that way. I do not refuse to drink stagnant water and seek running water because I think it is best for my bodily health to do so, but because I like the taste of running water and not of stagnant water. I do not refuse grass, green fruit, and decayed vegetables and seek beefsteak, ripe fruit and fresh vegetables merely or principally because the former are injurious and the latter beneficial to my bodily health. I decide on what I shall eat and drink according as it pleases or displeases me in the eating. The lower animals probably never do anything for the sake of the preservation and furtherance of their bodies, but their instincts guide them so accurately that it seems to us they must do some of these things with that in view. They choose the right food, the right drink, the right com-

The Instinct to Preserve and Further the Material Possessions

panions, etc., etc., because these things seem pleasant to them.

Herbert Spencer was of the opinion that mankind could follow instinct in the choice of food, drink, rest, exercise, temperature, etc., and that under normal conditions the choice would be such as would most certainly conduce to the highest preservation and development of the body. He believed that our instincts are so strong and so true that, when not perverted, they will act wisely in the presence of the appropriate stimuli, and that the bodily interests will best be furthered by passively following such instincts. He would hold that if that which is good for the body be presented in the proper light, we shall, of necessity, choose it and make the appropriate effort to secure it.

Food Instincts

If I think anything would taste good, I cannot keep from desiring it. I do not stop to consider whether it would be good for me or not. If it tastes good, that is sufficient. Nature has provided me with an instinctive desire to eat any and everything that tastes good, and, in general, such an instinct works wholly good. I am a reasoning creature, and it might be supposed that I would select from the different foods those which were best for my health, irrespective of their tastes. I find that my instinct is stronger than my reason in choosing what I shall eat. In the advertisement of Karo (No. 1) is this sentence: ". . . it makes you eat," and also this: ". . . gives a relish you can't resist." I should buy Karo at once if I believed it would be so enticing that it would make me go contrary to my reason and eat it even if my better judgment told me I should not. If I had been afflicted for years with indigestion I might do otherwise, but most persons have not yet been thus afflicted, and I feel confident that food advertisements have greatly improved during recent years, for they

No. 1.— An appeal to the instinct of bodily preservation.

are emphasizing more and more the taste of the food, and are making health qualities secondary, while price is being emphasized less.

The sense organs (the organs of sight, sound, taste, smell, temperature and touch) are the guardians of the body, and whatever appears good to these sentinels is instantly desired, and ordinarily such things tend to the preservation and furtherance of the welfare of the body, but we choose them simply because they appear pleasing and not for ulterior ends.

My clothes are in a special sense *mine*. We come to think of them almost as of our very bodies. How a small child will cry if his hat blows off or is taken! In our modern forms of civilization this instinct is weakened by the fact that we have so many clothes and change them so often that we hardly have time to become attached to any article of raiment before it is discarded. The close personal attachment which we have for our clothing is beautifully brought out by Professor James: "We so appropriate our clothes and identify ourselves with them that there are few of us who, if asked to choose between having a beautiful body, clad in raiment perpetually shabby and having an ugly form always spotlessly attired, would not hesitate a moment."

Clothing Instinct

We are all greatly attracted by the protection and ornamentation supplied by clothing. The amount of time which most women and some men spend on the subject of dress might seem absurd to a critic, but such are our human ways, and they seem good to us. Magazines devoted to fashions, shop-windows decorated with beautiful garments, advertisements of clothing — all these have an unending attraction for us. Clothing advertisements are read with avidity, and it has been discovered that all forms of clothing can be advertised with profit by means of the printed page.

The most careful observers of the actions of bees assure us that the little industrious bee gathers and stores away the honey simply because she enjoys the process, and not because she foresees the necessity for the honey which will come upon her during the wintry months. To say that the young bee has a prophetic insight of the coming winter is to attribute to it wisdom which is far above human wisdom.

Hoarding and Proprietary Instinct

Likewise the squirrel is said to collect nuts and store them away simply because that is the very action which is in itself more delightful than any other possible action. The squirrel does not store the nuts so that he will have them to eat during the winter, but when the winter comes on and nothing better is at hand of course he will eat them. If he had not stored them he would have starved during the winter, but he did not store them in order that he might not be reduced to starvation. As far as the individual squirrel is concerned, it was purely accidental that his storing the nuts provided against starvation.

There are many species of animals which thus collect and store away articles, and in some cases—in an unusual environment—the results are very peculiar. Professor Silliman thus describes the hoardings of a wood-rat in California made in an empty stove of an unoccupied house:

"I found the outside to be composed entirely of spikes, all laid with symmetry, so as to present the points of the nails outward. In the center of this mass was the nest, composed of finely divided fibers of hemp-packing. Interlaced with the spikes were the following: About two dozen knives, forks, and spoons; all the butcher's knives, three in number; a large carving-knife, fork and steel; several large plugs of tobacco, an old purse containing some silver, matches and tobacco; nearly all the tools from the tool-closets, with several large augers, all of which must have been transported some distance, as they were originally stored in different parts of the house. The outside casing of a silver watch was disposed of in one part of the pile, the glass of the same watch in another, and the works in still another."

There are very few persons who at some time in their lives have not made a collection of some sort. The little girls who make collections of buttons become exceedingly enthusiastic in their endeavors to make large collections, and, of course, if possible, to secure the most beautiful. If all the girls of the neighborhood are making collections too, the interest is greatly heightened. It is rather remarkable how all the children of a neighborhood may become interested in collecting such things as cancelled postage-stamps. Such a thing would hardly be possible if the children did not have an instinctive desire to make collections.

Making collections and hoarding is not confined to children, but is common to all adults. Occasionally some individual becomes absorbed in the process more than others and the results seem to us to be ludicrous, but they are instructive rather than ludicrous. The following is a description of the hoardings of a miser's den which was emptied by the Boston City Board of Health:

"He gathered old newspapers, wrapping-paper, incapacitated umbrellas, canes, pieces of common wire, cast-off clothing, empty barrels, pieces of iron, old bones, battered tinware, fractured pots, and bushels of such miscellany as is to be found only at the city 'dump.' The empty barrels were filled, shelves were filled, every hole and corner was filled, and in order to make more storage-room, 'the hermit' covered his store-room with a network of ropes, and hung the ropes as full as they could hold of his curious collections. There was nothing one could think of that wasn't in that room. As a wood-sawyer, the old man had never thrown away a saw-blade or a wood-buck. The bucks were rheumatic and couldn't stand up, and the saw-blades were worn down to almost nothing in the middle. Some had been actually worn in two, but the ends were carefully saved and stored away. As a coal-heaver, the old man had never cast off a worn-out basket, and there were dozens of the remains of the old things, patched up with canvas and rope-yarns in the store-room. There were at least two dozen old hats, fur, cloth, silk and straw, etc."

The man who could make such a collection as this is a miser, and he is despised for being such. He had too great a zeal for collecting and hoarding, and he allowed this zeal to obliterate the other possible interests of life. We all seem inclined to keep bits of useless finery and pieces of useless apparatus. The desire is often not yielded to, and the objects are thrown away because their presence becomes a nuisance. We all like to collect money, and the fact that it is useful and that others are making collections too merely tends to increase the instinctive desire to collect. The octogenarian continues to collect money with unabated zeal, although he may be childless, and the chief dread of his life is that his despised relatives may secure his money when he is gone. He does not desire that which money will secure, but the obtaining and holding the money is sufficient stimulus to him, even if every acquired dollar makes his difficulties greater by adding new responsibilities. No miser is aware of the fact that he collects for the pleasure he gets out of the collecting and the keeping. He imagines that he collects these things because of their usefulness. He may think that each thing he collects will come handy in some emergency; but that is not the ground of his collecting, although it may increase the tendency, and also make it seem reasonable to himself. It might be insulting to a business man to tell him that he was laboring for money merely because of the pleasure he receives in the gathering and keeping of it. Indeed, such a statement would ordinarily be but partially true, for, although the proprietary instinct may play a part, it certainly is not a complete explanation. All persons everywhere are tempted by a possibility of gain.

Our proprietary instincts may be made use of by the advertiser in many ways. The irresponsible advertiser has been able to play upon this instinct of the public by offering something for nothing, as is so frequently done in the cheaper forms of advertising media. The remarkable thing about this is that the public should be deluded by such a pretense. The desire to gain seems to overcome the better judgment of the more ignorant public and they become the victims of all sorts of treachery. The reputable advertiser should not disregard this instinct, and might often make it possible to minister to it with great profit, both to himself and to the public, which he might thus interest in what he has to offer. The following advertisement of the American Reserve Bond Co. (No. 2) is an attempt to appeal to this instinct.

The Hunting Instinct

Why will a man endure hardship for days, endanger his life, and incur great expense, merely for the chance of a shot at a poor inoffensive deer? It certainly is not because of the value of the venison or of the hide. It is not uncommon for a sportsman to give away his game as soon as he has killed it. What he wanted was the pleasure of killing the game. Why will a man wade in streams from morning till night, or hold a baited hook for hours in the burning sun? It certainly is not because fish are valuable; neither does he do it because he believes that it is good for his health. While engaged in the act he is perfectly indifferent to his health, and such a thought would be incongruous to the whole situation. We like to hunt and to fish because we have inherited the hunting instinct from remote ancestors. For the civilized man such an instinct is often worthless, but to our ancestors it was necessary for the preservation of life. The charm which a gun or a fishing tackle has for

No. 2.—A successful appeal to the hoarding instinct.

a civilized man is a most remarkable thing. The annual sale of rifles, revolvers, fishing tackle, fishing boats, etc., is beyond anything which could be attributed to their practical need. The hunting instinct shows itself in our fiendish desire for conflict. The more ferocious the animal and the "gamier" the fish, the greater is our delight. The conflict may be with a man, and then the fiercer the struggle the better we like it. A street-brawl never fails to attract a crowd. The prize-fighter is always accompanied by the admiring glances of the populace. The accounts of atrocious crimes are read by those who are ashamed to confess it.

The advertiser of guns, revolvers, fishing tackle, etc., meets with a ready response from the youth because he appeals directly to his powerful instincts. The following advertisement of Stevens Rifles (No. 3) is a good illustration of an appeal to the hunting instinct:

No. 3.—A successful appeal to the hunting instinct.

The constructive instinct shows itself in a well-known manner in the bee and the beaver. The same instinct is common to man, but the results are not so uniform. We all like to construct things; if they are already constructed then we want to remodel or improve them. There is hardly a man who at least once has not been conscious of a strong desire to build a house. If he purchases one already constructed, then he is not content till he has remodeled it in some way. Indeed, if he has built it himself he may make improvements upon it annually. If it is not so that he can make more changes the home loses interest, and is likely to be abandoned. As soon as the possibility of improving a home has passed it seems that both the host and hostess seek excuses for going north or south or traveling abroad.

The Constructing Instinct

In our urban civilization the men are deprived of one of the great pleasures of life. We are shut in as children, and are not allowed to "make a muss" by our attempts at construction, and in our maturity the instinct is held in check by lack of exercise. If we had some opportunity to make things with our hands we should secure the best possible form of recreation and diversion from the anxieties of business life. The women have all sorts of fancy-work with which they may amuse themselves. Manual-training and domestic science are offering an opportunity to school-children to use their hands and give expression to this instinctive desire to construct things.

The advertiser can appeal in many ways to this instinct, and is sure to find ready attention and a willingness to pay for the opportunity to exercise this much-neglected instinct. The following advertisement of Golden Fleece yarn is such that it makes a woman's fingers tingle with a desire to crochet.

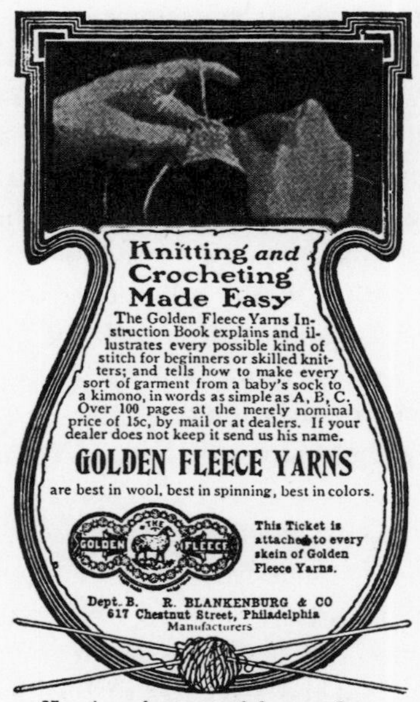

No. 4.— A successful appeal to the constructing instinct.

The Parental Instinct

One of the most striking instincts in the entire animal kingdom is that of maternal love. The mother of one of the higher animals or of the human infant is willing to sacrifice all for her infant. The description which a German by the name of Schneider wrote of this instinct is clearly German, but is an excellent description of the facts:

"As soon as a wife becomes a mother her whole thought and feeling, her whole being, is altered. Until then she had only thought of her own well-being, of the satisfaction of her vanity; the whole world appeared made only for her; everything that went on about her was only noticed so far as it had personal reference to her; she asked of everyone that he should appear interested in her, pay her the requisite attention, and as far as possible fulfil her wishes. Now, however, the center of the world is no longer herself, but her child. She does not think of her own hunger; she must first be sure that the child is fed. It is nothing to her that she herself is tired and needs rest, so long as she sees that the child's sleep is disturbed; the moment it stirs she awakes, though far stronger noises fail to arouse her now. She has, in one word, transformed her entire egotism to the child, and lives only in it. Thus, at least, it is in all unspoiled, naturally bred mothers, and thus it is with all the higher animal mothers.

"She does not herself know why she is so happy, and why the look of the child and the care of it are so agreeable, any more than the young man can give an account of why he loves the maiden, and is so happy when she is near. Few mothers, in caring for their children, think of the proper purpose of maternal love for the preservation of the species. Such a thought may arise in the father's mind; seldom in that of the mother. The latter feels only that it is an everlasting delight to hold the being which she has brought forth protectingly in her arms, to dress it, to wash it, to rock it to sleep, or to still its hunger." (Condensed from James' Psychology.)

Anything that will administer to the needs of the child is a necessity in the eyes of the mother. The matter of expense has to be considered by many mothers, but as men think lightly of expense when satisfying their hunting instincts, so the mothers look upon expense as of secondary importance when supplying the needs of their children. An article which in any way administers to the appearance or comfort of children needs but to be brought to the attention of mothers and it is sure to be desired by them with a desire which is much more than a passing fancy, for it is enforced by the maternal instinct as inherited from countless generations. Advertisers are very successful in appealing to this instinct. The advertisement of Cream of Wheat (No. 5) is but one of many advertisements which thus appeal most forcibly to all mothers.

The Instincts Affecting the "Social Self."

No one chooses solitude for a long period of time. We prefer the best of companionship, but in the absence of the best we accept the best available. Robinson Crusoe took great comfort in the companionship of his man Friday. Solitary confinement is a severer form of punishment than any other employed by civilized nations. We are gregarious and want to be able to see other human beings. Not

No. 5.—A successful attempt to appeal to the parental instinct.

only do we want to see others, but we want to be seen and noticed by them. Why should I care for myself as I appear in the minds of other people? It is not necessary for me to explain the origin of such a regard for the opinion of others, but it would hardly have been possible for the race to have developed without such a preference. Indeed, if an individual should become wholly oblivious to the opinion of others, it is doubtful whether he would be able to survive for any considerable period of time.

The young man seems compelled to attempt to be at his best before the young lady, but he does not know why. The young boy always tries to " show off " in the presence of young girls. It is often ridiculous that he should do so, and he does not know why he is doing it. When he comes into the presence of the young girl he seems compelled to undertake something *bizarre* which is sure to attract her attention. We are all afflicted as the young man and the boy. We consult not only our preference but also the opinion of others in purchasing our clothes and our homes, and in choosing our friends and our professions. We seem compelled to strive for those things which will make us rise in the estimation of others, and in purchasing and choosing we select those things which are approved by those whose esteem we most covet. If a particular style of clothing is preferred by the class of society whose esteem we court, that is a great argument in favor of such goods. It is possible for the advertiser of all classes of clothing to take advantage of this characteristic of human nature and to present his garments as if they were being worn by this preferred set. Indeed, at the present time, there are many classes of goods which are being presented as the preferred of the " veritable swells." When, on the

No. 6.— I feel that by buying a Gage hat I should be brought into the social class of these ladies.

contrary, an advertiser represents his goods as that preferred by a despised class of individuals, the effect produced is distinctly harmful.

The reproduced advertisement of Gage Millinery (No. 6) makes us believe that by selecting a Gage hat we should be brought, in the eyes of our acquaintances, into the class of persons here represented.

The advertisements of Regal Shoes (No. 7) and of White Star Coffee (No. 8) make us avoid them, for

No. 7.—I refuse to admire the Regal shoe, for it will bring me into the class with this fellow.

we do not want to be considered as in the class with frogs and peasants. The coffee and shoes may be all right, but if, by using them, I am to be thought less of by my acquaintances, I will have none of them.

Our limbs would be useless unless with them we inherited a desire to exercise them. We do not exercise our limbs in order that we may develop them; but,

The Instincts Affecting the Psychical Nature

nevertheless, the chief value of such exercise may be the development of the limbs. With every organ we inherit a desire to exercise it in a way which makes for its development. The child's mind is but a potential affair. It must be exercised in order that it may develop. If the child exer-

No. 8.— A poor advertisement. What would my acquaintances think of me if I preferred the same brand of coffee as that which delights the frogs?

cised only when it realized that such exercise was necessary for the development of the body, it is quite certain that there would never be a fully developed adult again.

Along with our bodies we have inherited a psychical nature with all its diversified possibilities. The psychical nature is, however, but little more than a possibility which needs vigorous exercise for its realization.

We have a moral nature which, in the beginning,

is in the crudest possible form, but we have an inherited liking for the consideration of moral questions. This consideration may be of the actions of the hero in a story, of the nation's leaders, of a seller of merchandise, or of a personal friend. Such consideration of actions of others is most beneficial in the development of the moral sense, and when moral questions are presented in a true light, they are intensely interesting to all classes of persons.

Socrates believed that all persons would prefer the right whenever they saw it, and that all evil actions were from ignorance. Such a view is evidently an exaggeration, but we certainly do prefer what we regard to be the right, and reject what we regard to be the wrong. This is especially true in regard to the actions of others. We are disgusted and repulsed by what we regard as wrong in others. If an advertiser's argument, illustration and condition of purchase are such that they offend the moral sense of the reader, the advertisement is of little or no value. It may be difficult to appeal especially to the moral judgment of the possible customer in presenting most goods, but any offense to such a moral judgment must be scrupulously avoided. In the advertisements of books, periodicals and schools, the moral judgment can safely be counted on. Whether the religious nature be developed from the moral or not, it certainly is true that the two are very closely connected, and that they must both be regarded with care by the advertiser, whether they be appealed to directly by the advertisement or not. The avidity with which we seek things which appeal to our religious nature is illustrated by a circumstance related in the September, 1904, issue of the *Atlantic Monthly*. A book was offered to the public with the title, "The Wonders of Nature," but the sales were disappointing. The title was changed to "The Wonders of Nature, the Architecture of God," and the sales were immediately increased and a second edition was necessary.

We have even as children an embryonic, esthetic nature. Things beautiful have a fascinating effect upon the unperverted individual. We need but to have objects of beauty brought to our attention and we desire them without being taught their desirability.

Furthermore, the beautiful affects us without our knowledge of the fact. We stop and look at a beautiful advertisement, but may not be aware that it is the beauty that attracts us at all. The best works of art are such that the attention is drawn wholly to what is represented, and not to the manner of the representation. The advertisement which is most artistic may be one which never affects the public as being artistic at all, but it is the one which will be most effective in impressing the possible customer. One reason why so much attention is given to the advertising pages of our magazines is that they are so artistic.

We have an intellectual nature, but in the case of the child the intellect is little more than a spark which, however, is sufficient to indicate the presence of that which may be developed into a great light. The child is prompted by curiosity to examine everything that comes into its environment. It tears its toys to pieces that it may learn of their construction. At a later age the youth takes delight in the acquisition of knowledge independent of the utility of such knowledge. The curiosity of the human race is the salvation of its intellect, and at the same time makes a convenient point of attack for the advertiser. The public wants to know what is offered for sale. It wants to hear the story which the advertiser has to tell. There are other stories to hear, and the advertiser must not have the most uninteresting one if he expects to take advantage of this instinctive desire of the individual to become acquainted with all novel objects and to learn all he can concerning new aspects of familiar ones.

Occasionally this characteristic of curiosity may be made use of by the advertiser in what might seem to be an absurd manner, and yet the results be good. As an illustration, observe the reproduced advertisement of "What did the woggle bug say?" (No. 9). This advertisement seems to be extremely absurd, and yet, in some way, it has been able to arouse the curiosity of many readers, and it is quite possible that it has been a successful advertisement.

We have seen above that we have instinctive responses to act for the preservation and furtherance of (1) our bodies, clothes, homes, personal property and family (also the hunting and constructing instincts which are more complex than others of this class);

(2) ourselves as we exist in the minds of others; (3) our mental faculties. We have seen that to secure action along these lines it is not necessary to show the value of such action or the necessity of it, but merely to present the proper stimulus, and the action is forthcoming immediately. The advertiser should study hu-

No. 9.— An advertising freak designed to arouse curiosity.

man nature to discover these hidden springs of action. He desires to produce the maximum of action along a certain line with the minimum of effort and expense to himself. If he can find a method whereby his efforts are seconded by some of the most powerful of the human instincts, his task will be simplified to the extreme. The discovery of such a method is a task for the leaders of the profession of advertising.

VI
SUGGESTION

What is Suggestion?

THE mental process known as "Suggestion" is in bad repute because, in the popular mind, it has too often been associated on the one hand with hypnotism and on the other with indelicacy and vulgarity. Hypnotism in the hands of the scientist or of the fakir is well known to be a form of suggestion. A story which does not specifically depart from that which conforms to the standards of propriety but which is so constructed that it leads the hearers to conceptions that are "off color" is said to be suggestive. In this way it has come to pass that the whole subject of suggestion has been passed by with less consideration than is due it.

There is no uniformity in the meanings that are attached to the term *suggestion* even among the most careful writers. If I were sitting in my office and considering the advisability of beginning a certain enterprise, I might say that one idea "suggested" a second and this second a third, etc. A scientific definition would not allow this use of the term but would substitute the expression "called up" for "suggested." Thus I should say that one idea "called up" the second, etc. *Suggestion must be brought about by a second person or an object.* In my musings and deliberations I should not say that one idea suggested another, but if the same idea were called forth at the instigation of a second person or upon the presentation of an object, I should then call it suggestion — if it met the second essential condition of suggestion. This second condition is that *the resulting conception, conclusion or action must follow with less than the normal amount of deliberation.* Suggestion is thus a relative term, and in many instances it might be difficult to say whether or not a particular act was suggestion. If the act followed a normal amount of consideration after a normal time for deliberation, it would not be suggestion, while if the same act followed too abruptly or with too little consideration it might be a true case of suggestion.

Universality of Suggestion

Every normal individual is subject to the influence of suggestion. Every idea of which we think is all too liable to be held for truth, and every thought of an action which enters our minds is likely to result in such action. I do not think first of walking and then make up my mind to walk. The very thought of walking will inevitably lead to the act unless I stop the process by the thought of standing still. If I think of an object to the east of me my whole body sways slightly in that direction. Such action is so slight that we ordinarily do not discover it without the aid of accurate recording instruments. Almost all so-called mind-reading exhibitions are nothing but demonstrations of the fact that every thought which we think expresses itself in some outward action.

Thought is dynamic in its very nature and every idea of an action tends to produce that action.

The most perfect working of suggestion is to be seen under hypnosis and in crowds. In hypnosis the subject holds every idea presented as true, and every idea suggested is acted out with no hesitation whatever. Here the mind is so narrowed by the artificial sleep that no contradictory or inhibiting idea arises, and hence no idea can seem absurd and no action seems out of place. There is no possible criticism or deliberation and so we have the extreme case of susceptibility to suggestion.

The effect of a crowd upon an individual approaches that of the hypnotizer. The individual is affected by every member of the crowd and the influence becomes so overpowering that it can hardly be resisted. If the crowd is a "lynching party" the whole atmosphere is one of revenge, and everywhere is suggested the idea of "lynch the culprit." This idea is presented on all sides. It can be read from the faces and actions of the individuals and is heard in their cries. No other idea has a chance to arise in consciousness and hence this one idea, being dynamic, leads to its natural consequences.

Reasoning Not Universal

It was once supposed that suggestion was something abnormal and that reason was the common attribute of men. To-day we are finding that suggestion is of universal application to all persons, while reason is a process which is exceptional, even among the wisest. We reason rarely, but act under suggestion constantly.

There has been a great agitation of late among advertisers for "reason why" copy. This agitation has had some value, but it is easily over-emphasized. Occasionally customers are persuaded and convinced, but more frequently they make their purchases because the act is suggested at the psychological moment. Suggestion and persuasion are not antagonistic; both should be kept in mind. However, in advertising, suggestion should not be subordinated to persuasion but should be supplemented by it. The actual effect of modern advertising is not so much to convince as to suggest. The individual swallowed up by a crowd is not aware of the fact that he is not exercising a normal amount of deliberation. His actions appear to him to be the result of reason, although the idea, as presented, is not criticised at all and no contradictory or inhibiting idea has any possibility of arising in his mind. In the same way we think that we are performing a deliberate act when we purchase an advertised commodity, while in fact we may never have deliberated upon the subject at all. The idea is suggested by the advertisement, and the impulsiveness of human nature enforces the suggested idea, hence the desired result follows in a way unknown to the purchaser.

Some time ago a tailor in Chicago was conducting a vigorous advertising campaign. I did not suppose that his advertising was having any influence upon me. Some months after the advertising had begun I went into the tailor's shop and ordered a suit. While in the shop I happened to fall into conversation with the proprietor and he asked me if a friend had recommended him to me. I replied that such was the case. Thereupon I tried to recall who the friend was and finally came to the conclusion that this shop had never been recommended to me at all. I had seen his advertisements for months and from them had formed an idea of the shop. Later, I forgot where I had received my information and assumed that I had received it from a friend who patronized the shop. I discovered that all I knew of the shop I had learned from advertisements and I doubt very much whether I ever read any of the advertisements further than the display type. Doubtless many other customers would have given the same reply even though, as in my case, no friend had spoken to them concerning the shop.

Effective Forms of Suggestion

Ideas which have the greatest suggestive power are those presented to us by the actions of other persons. The second most effective class is probably the ideas suggested by the words of our companions. Advertisements that are seen frequently are difficult to distinguish in their force from ideas which are secured from the words of our friends. Advertising thus becomes a great social illusion. We attribute to our social environment that which in reality has been secured from the advertisements which we have seen so often that we forget the source of the information.

Street railway advertising is especially effective at this point because the suggestion is presented so frequently that we soon forget the source of the suggestions and end by attributing it to the advice of friends.

In advertising some commodities argumentation is of more importance than suggestion, and for such things booklets and other similar forms of advertising are the most effective. Such commodities are, however, the exception and not the rule. In the most successful advertising argumentation and forms of reasoning are not disregarded, but the emphasis is put upon suggestion. Inasmuch as more of our actions are induced by suggestion than by argumentation, advertising conforms, in this particular, to the psychological situation. It puts the emphasis where the most can be accomplished and subordinates those mental processes which hold a second place in determining our actions.

As stated above, those suggestions are the most powerful which we receive from the actions and words of other persons. The successful advertiser seems to have worked upon this hypothesis in constructing many advertisements. He has also taken advantage of the fact that we soon forget the person who originally suggested the idea and become subject to illusions upon the matter. Thus, in the reproduced advertisements of Jap-a-lac (No. 1), as I see this young lady using Jap-a-lac the suggestion to do the same thing is overpowering. Many a woman who has looked at these pictures has been immediately overcome by a desire

No. 1.— The actions of this young lady are compelling in their suggestive power.

to do the same thing and has put her desire into execution. If I had seen these and similar cards for a few months, even though I had never seen anyone actually using the paint, I should assume that "every one is using Jap-a-lac." The suggestion would thereupon be in an extreme form and be liable to cause me to imitate what I assumed every one else was doing. As a matter of fact I *was* affected in just this manner. When occasion arose to purchase some paint for household use I called for Jap-a-lac under the assumption that I had seen it used frequently. The can looked familiar, and it seemed to me that I was running no risks, for Jap-a-lac had been a household commodity for years. Soon after the purchase I began to write this chapter and I am unable to recall any instance of having seen Jap-a-lac in use. I had seen pictures of the Jap-a-lac paint can and had seen pictures of persons using the paint, but I know of no other source of information concerning this paint, although at the time of the purchase of the paint my knowledge of it seemed to me perfectly adequate. Apparently I had never heard an argument in favor of the paint but had acted upon mere suggestion. Women are, in general, more susceptible to suggestion than men, and I feel sure that many women are convinced of the adequacy of this paint by these same advertisements, reproduced above, even though nothing more than the display and the picture is noticed.

It seems that no form of action can be suggested by an advertisement that does not successfully challenge the reader to do what is proposed. The suggested idea haunts one and even though the action may be absurd, it is difficult to resist. The three following advertisements have all appeared in street-cars and have met with phenomenal success. Many persons

No. 2.— A suggestion to rub your finger.

doubtless feel the suggestion to be irresistible to rub the end of the first finger when looking at this advertisement of Lucas's Tinted Gloss Paint.

No. 3.— A suggestion to solve this.

What could be more absurd than Westerfeld's advertisement? The fact that this advertisement was highly successful is sufficient justification for its use. Kerr's studio was flooded with answers to the suggestion of "Guess who?" The suggestions in these three advertisements lead the readers to desire to act in the ways suggested, and that of necessity leads to a careful reading of the entire advertisements.

As stated above, the words of our friends have strong suggestive power. We are not cold, logical machines, who take data in and then, by a logical

No. 4.—The action suggested by this advertisement makes it effective.

process, come to a reasonable conclusion. On the contrary, we are so highly susceptible to suggestion that the words of our companions are ordinarily held for true and the actions proposed by them are hastily carried out. The suggestiveness of the words of companions is a value available to the advertiser. He

No. 5.— The venerable doctor seems to make the suggestion.

places before the public a statement and then, to give it greater suggestive power, he shows the likeness of a person whose face indicates the possession of a judgment we should be willing to take. The advertiser does not state that the words are those of the person depicted, but this relationship seems to be suggested and it adds greatly to the value of the advertisement. Thus in the reproduced advertisement of Postum Food Coffee the picture of the venerable doctor becomes associated in our minds with the statement, "If coffee don't agree, use Postum Food Coffee." Later these words seem to have issued from a responsible person and come to have undue weight with us all. Likewise

No. 6.— The washerwoman seems to recommend Arrow collars.

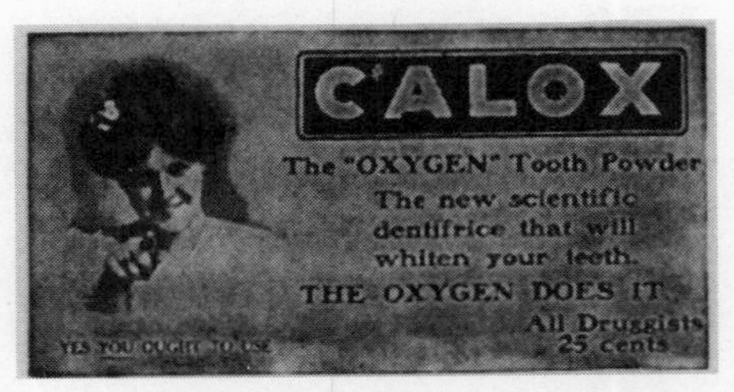

No. 7.—The portrait doubles the suggestive power of this advertisement.

in the reproduced advertisement of Arrow collars the genial washerwoman seems to assure us that "Arrow Collars don't shrink in the wash." In the case of the

Calox advertisement I am convinced when this beautiful girl points her finger at me and seems to say, "Yes, you ought to use Calox." As I happen to need more tooth powder just now, I don't wait for further evidence but accept uncritically the words which she is represented as using. When we stop to think of it, it is absurd to place additional credence in these words of the advertiser simply because of the presence of an appropriate picture, but the absurdity of the situation

HAND SAPOLIO
by a method of its own cleans the pores, aids the natural changes of the skin, and imparts new vigor and life.
Don't argue, Don't infer, Try it!
It's a lightning change from office to parlor with Hand Sapolio.
SHOULD BE ON EVERY WASHSTAND

No. 8.—A good advertisement in which suggestion is subordinated to argumentation.

does not detract from the practical value of such forms of suggestion.

Many forms of suggestion, in addition to those presented above, are available to the advertiser. There is also no necessary divorce between suggestion and the presentation of arguments. Indeed, the application of the two in the same advertisement often increases the value of each. Thus in the reproduced advertisement of Hand Sapolio (No. 8) the direct suggestion, "Hand Sapolio should be on every washstand," is strengthened by the "reasons why," and the reasons why are strengthened by this suggestion.

These reproduced advertisements are presented as mere illustrations of a few of the many ways in which suggestion may be used by the advertiser. We have but to consider the millions of persons who at least glance at advertisements, to be impressed by the possibilities opened to the man who can present his advertisement in a form that suggests powerfully the purchase or use of his commodity.

VII
THE WILL: AN ANALYSIS

Knowing, Feeling, Willing

DURING all the waking hours of the day there is something about which we are *thinking;* we have a particular tone of *feeling,* and there is something for which we are *striving.* We know something, we feel somehow, and we strive for something not yet attained. Knowing, feeling and willing are the three universal aspects of all our mental activities. As I sit in my chair I am conscious of the furniture in the room, the line of thought which I am carrying out and the necessity of completing my task in a given time; I feel pleased with the comfort of the situation and the excitement of composition; I am putting forth activity of will in striving to accomplish a certain end and to express myself on a typewriter. Sometimes our condition is one of intense feeling, at another it is primarily intellectual grasp of a situation and at other times it is especially a putting forth the will in attempting to accomplish some end or to reach some conclusion. Although each of the three aspects of consciousness may for a time predominate yet it is probable that all three activities are present at all moments of our conscious existence.

Under the will may be included all the *active* processes of the mind. This activity may express itself either in bodily movements or in some such mental processes as attention or volition. Under the bodily activities are such as impulsive, instinctive and voluntary actions. At this time it will be well to confine our attention to but a part of these activities of the will, viz., voluntary actions.

A definition of volition would not make the subject any clearer to us, but here the term is used in an untechnical sense and includes such things as decision, choice, voluntary actions, and all actions performed after consideration. It includes a mental process and the resultant, bodily activity.

It is probably true that a majority of our actions are performed without such consideration, but it is because of the existence of voluntary action that the advertiser finds it necessary to proceed logically and to appeal to the reason of his customer.

A careful consideration of the elemental processes involved in such actions is of great advantage in enabling the advertiser to bring about the decision desired.

Voluntary Action Analyzed

Voluntary actions may be analyzed into (*a*) an idea of two or more attainable ends, (*b*) an idea of the means to attain these ends, (*c*) a feeling of the value or worthiness of the different ends, (*d*) a comparison of the values of the different ends and of the difficulties of the means and, finally, (*e*) a choosing of one of the ends and striving to attain it.

These five processes in a voluntary action may be illustrated as follows: (*a*) I think of a suit that I might buy, the trip that I might take, and of the debt that I might pay; (*b*) I think of the trouble of going to the tailor shop, the inconvenience of waiting for the train, and the distance to be covered to reach the creditor; (*c*) I feel in imagination the pleasure of possessing the new suit, the delights connected with the trip, and the satisfaction of having the debt paid; (*d*) I compare the difficulties of possessing each and the pleasures derivable from the possession; (*e*) I decide to take the trip and start for the ticket office.

If this is a correct analysis of voluntary action the question which naturally arises in the mind of the advertiser is this: What can be done to cause the largest number of persons to decide in favor of my particular goods? Suppose that the article of merchandise under consideration be a piano: now how may the advertiser proceed in accordance with the analysis presented above? (*a*) The piano must be brought before the public in such a manner that the idea of it will be clear and distinct in the minds of the potential purchasers. (*b*) The public must be informed exactly what is necessary to secure the piano. (*c*) The piano must be presented in such a manner that its value seems great. (*d*) The value of the piano must be presented in such a way that, when compared with other forms of action, the purchase of the piano seems the most desirable. The means of securing the piano must be made to appear easy. (*e*) Pressure must be brought to bear to cause immediate decision

Application to Advertising

and action on the part of the public in favor of the particular piano.

Elaborations of each of these five points will suggest themselves to any thoughtful advertiser. That the idea of the piano may be clear and distinct (*a*) illustrations may be used to advantage; the language used should conform to the mode of thinking of the public appealed to; the type used should be easily read; the description should be as brief as is possible for completeness of presentation of essential features. In order that the public may know exactly how to secure the piano (*b*) the exact cost must be presented; the method of sending the money, the delivery and setting up in the home might well be included in the statement of the advertisement. The feeling of value may be awakened for the piano (*c*) by advertising it in the highest class of media, by having a beautiful advertisement, by emphasizing the elegance of the instrument and the perfection of the tone, by indicating what a joy it is in a home, and by any other means which would tend to associate the piano with feelings of pleasure. It is assumed that other pianos will be considered by the possible purchasers and that when others are considered they will suffer by comparison (*d*). That this may be true it will be necessary to describe the strong points of the piano in such a way that the value of the piano seems great, and the cost of it and the means of securing it seem less burdensome than those connected with competing pianos. That the choice may be made at once and effort put forth to secure the piano (*e*) reasons for avoiding delay might be presented or the suggestion to action might be so strong that the tendency to procrastinate would be overcome.

Although every customer who is induced to select any particular line of goods after consideration must inevitably perform the five processes as described, and although an ideal advertisement would be so constructed that it would assist the customer in completing each of the five processes, yet it is not to be assumed that each advertisement should be constructed so that it would be well adapted to promote each of the five processes.

On the other hand, it is quite true that many advertisements are ineffective because the writer has not paid attention to these fundamental psychological processes of voluntary actions.

In the reproduced advertisement of Triscuit (No. 1) the first step of the act of volition (*a*) is emphasized.

Adequate Description of Goods Advertised

This advertisement gives the reader a clear and vivid idea of the product advertised. No one can read the advertisement without knowing what the product is made of, how it looks, how it is manufactured and what it is good for.

The reproduced advertisement of Holbrook's Sauce (No. 2) occupied the cover page in a British magazine which is about twelve by sixteen inches in size. In all this space nothing is shown or said which gives us an idea of the real nature of the product advertised. After examining this advertisement carefully I am still at a loss to know the real nature of the product. Such a use of space can be justified only on the assumption that the public is already familiar with the sauce, or that this is to be but a single link in the

No. 1.—Adequate description of goods, but inadequate as to method of securing them.

chain and that later or preceding advertisements supply what is deficient in this single advertisement.

Many an otherwise good advertisement is weakened because it gives no adequate idea of the means necessary for securing the goods advertised. The advertiser is so familiar with his goods and the means of securing them that he forgets that others know nothing of them. It is needless to reproduce any particular advertisement to illustrate this point. A large proportion of goods that are widely distributed

Method of Securing the Goods

No. 2.—Inadequate description of the goods and of the method of securing them.

are advertised on the assumption that everybody knows that they are to be secured at all dealers. It is not wise to assume any such knowledge on the part of the general public. In the advertisement of Triscuit no mention is made of the fact that it can be secured from all first-class grocers, and many persons assume that Triscuit can be had only at the address given at the

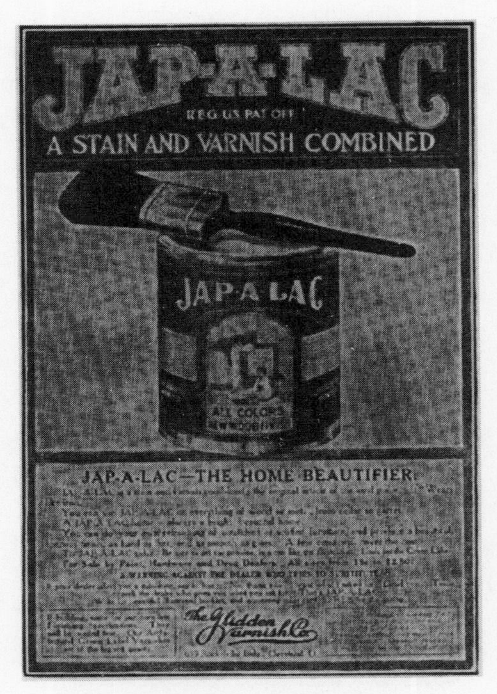

No. 3.— Adequate description of the method of securing the goods.

foot of the advertisement. In the advertisement of Holbrook's Sauce (No. 2) no address is given and nothing is said of the place where it can be secured. The writers of the advertisements have assumed that the public knows more of these goods than the facts warrant.

The reproduced advertisement of Jap-a-lac (No. 3) leaves no doubt in the mind of the public as to the means of securing the paint. "For sale by paint, hardware, drug dealers. All sizes from 15c to $2.50." This statement is sufficient for most persons, but not for all, and we find this statement in addition: "If your dealer does not keep Jap-a-lac, send us his name and 10c and we will send free sample." This advertisement gives us a clear idea of the means necessary for securing the advertised goods and hence facilitates the second process in a voluntary action and increases the chances of securing the desired action. No advertisement should ever appear which leaves any doubt in the minds of possible customers as to where and how the goods advertised can be secured. The absence of such information is very common and impresses the writer as one of the weakest points in modern advertising.

The third process in our analysis of voluntary action is the feeling of worthiness or value (*c*). It is not sufficient to have a clear idea of an end and a definite idea of the means of securing it unless there is an accompanying feeling of value. The advertiser is thus compelled to make his commodity appear valuable. This fact is accomplished by most advertisers but not by all. The reproduced advertisement of Nabisco (No. 4) presents the product as particularly

The Feeling of Worth

worthy. The advertisement is intrinsically beautiful. The cut and the copy harmonize completely. The young girl depicted could be described as "a fairy," and "airy lightness and exquisite composition" is

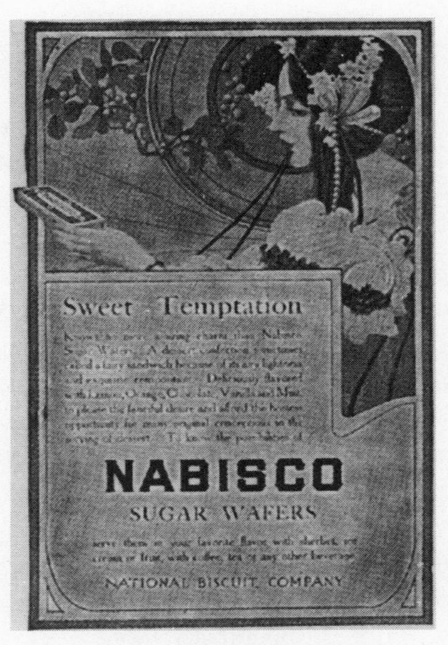

No. 4.—This advertisement arouses a feeling of appreciation.

characteristic of the entire cut. The copy appeals to our instinctive desires for savory viands in a most enticing manner, and also appeals to the feminine social instinct by the following words: ". . . to afford the hostess opportunity for many original conceptions in the serving of desserts." The greatest feeling of worth attaches itself to those things which are the objects of our most fundamental instinctive desires. A feeling of worth inevitably attaches itself to every savory viand, to every beautiful object, and to every agency which furthers our social instincts.

The fourth process in our analysis (*d*) is the comparison of competing ends as to value and means of acquisition. When an advertiser realizes that the public to which he is appealing will compare his goods with those of his competitor, he is tempted to resort to the questionable method of showing the weak points of his competitor's merchandise or method of sales. There may be instances in which this method is justifiable and even necessary, but ordinarily it is self-destructive. The act of comparison (*d*) is a process in volition that the advertiser should not seek to encourage. It is a hindrance to the advertiser and his function is to minimize it. If I, as an advertiser, am offering goods in competition with other goods, I know that my goods will be compared with the others, and it is my place to give the reader such a clear and vivid idea of my goods (*a*) and to make the means of securing them so plain (*b*) that my goods will not suffer by comparison. My purpose is best served by holding my goods up to the attention of the potential purchaser and not by emphasizing the weaknesses of those of my competitor. I must emphasize the strong points of my merchandise and especially those points

Treatment of Competing Goods

in which my goods are superior to competing goods, and in this way I get attention to those points at which my goods will gain by comparison.

Completing the Process

The last point in the analysis of the process of volition (*e*) is that of choosing one of the ends and striving to attain it. All the other stages of the process are but subsidiary to this. What can the advertiser do to secure or to facilitate this part of the process? It is a well-known psychological fact that at the moment of final decision all competing ideas are usually banished from the mind and attention is centered on the idea (the merchandise) which is chosen. At the moment of final choice we do not hold competing lines of action before us and then choose the one that seems the best. The process is one of elimination preceding the choice. We compare different lines of action and eliminate one after another till but one is left. This one has seemed better than the others and it is held to and acted upon. The acting upon it is often a part of the choice. The one line of action is before us and the very act of attending to the one idea results in the appropriate action. There may have been no conscious choice preceding the action but now that the action has commenced the competing ideas are kept from the mind and the action gets put into fulfillment. There are therefore two distinct things which the advertiser can do to facilitate this final step. In the first place he fills the mind of his potential customers with thoughts of his own particular goods and, in the second place, he suggests immediate action. The mind of the customer is filled by the processes described in (*a*), (*b*) and (*c*). Immediate action is suggested by (*b*) and by some such device as the return coupon, the direct command, etc. . (For a fuller discussion of this point see chapters V and VI of "The Theory of Advertising.") The advertiser who fails to state the method of securing his goods fails to give one of the strongest possible suggestions to action.

If it were even possible that every reader of the advertisement of Jap-a-lac already knew the price of it and where it could be secured, still the advertisement is strengthened by giving these details in that it gives the suggestion to action as nothing else could do. The suggestion to action might be strengthened by additional details but not by substituting for them.

VIII

THE WILL: VARIETY IN ACTION

Differences in Individuals

In the preceding chapter an analysis of a typical action was given without reference to the fact that actions are not ordinarily typical. No two acts are exactly alike. Individuals are different and employ divers methods in performing their acts. In the case of a single individual the most diverse methods are employed at different times and under different circumstances. The personal differences in methods of deciding questions and resultant actions has been so beautifully expressed by Professor William James that it seems useless to attempt any improvement upon his presentation of the five methods of deciding or choosing:

"The first method may be called the reasonable type. It is that of those cases in which the arguments for and against a given course seem gradually and almost insensibly to settle themselves in the mind and to end by leaving a clear balance in favor of one alternative, which alternative we then adopt without effort or constraint. . . . The conclusive reason for the decision in these cases usually is the discovery that we can refer the case to a *class* upon which we are accustomed to act unhesitatingly in a certain stereotyped way. . . . The moment we hit upon a conception which lets us apply some principle of action which is a fixed and stable part of our Ego, our state of doubt is at an end. Persons of authority, who have to make many decisions in the day, carry with them a set of heads of classification, each bearing its volitional consequence, and under these they seek as far as possible to range each new emergency as it occurs. It is where the emergency belongs to a species without precedent, to which consequently no cut-and-dried maxim will apply, that we feel most at a loss, and are distressed at the indeterminateness of our task. As soon, however, as we see our way to a familiar classification, we are at ease again. . . . The concrete dilemmas do not come to us with labels gummed on their backs. We may name them by many names. The wise man is he who succeeds in finding the name which suits the needs of the particular occasion best.

"A 'reasonable' character is one who has a store of stable and worthy ends, and who does not decide about an action till he has calmly ascertained whether it be ministerial or detrimental to any one of these. In the next two types of decision, the final fiat occurs before the evidence is all 'in.' It often happens that no paramount and authoritative reason for either course will come. Either seems a good, and there is no umpire to decide which should yield its place to the other. We grow tired of long hesitation and inconclusiveness, and the hour may come when we feel that even a bad decision is better than no decision at all. Under these conditions it will often happen that some accidental circumstance, supervening at a particular moment upon our mental weariness, will upset the balance in the direction of one of the alternatives, to which we then feel ourselves committed, although an opposite accident at the same time might have produced the opposite result.

"In the *second type* our feeling is to a great extent that of letting ourselves drift with a certain indifferent acquiescence in a direction accidentally determined *from without,* with the conviction that, after all, we might as well stand by this course as by the other, and that things are in any event sure to turn out sufficiently right.

"In the *third type* the determination seems equally accidental, but it comes from within, and not from without. It often happens, when the absence of imperative principles is perplexing and suspense distracting, that we find ourselves acting, as it were, automatically, and as if by a spontaneous discharge of our nerves, in the direction of one of the horns of the dilemma. But so exciting is this sense of motion after our intolerable pent-up state that we eagerly throw ourselves into it. 'Forward now!' we inwardly cry, 'though the heavens fall.'

"There is a *fourth form* of decision, which often ends deliberation as suddenly as the third form does. It comes when, in consequence of some outer experience or some inexplicable inward change, *we suddenly pass from the easy and careless to the sober and strenuous mood,* or possibly the other way. The whole scale of values of our motives and impulses then undergoes a change like that which a change of the observer's level produces on a view. The most sobering possible agents are objects of grief and fear. When one of these affects us, all 'light fantastic' notions lose their motive power, all solemn ones find theirs multiplied many fold. The consequence is an instant abandonment of the more trivial projects with which we had been dallying, and an instant practical acceptance of the more grim and earnest alternative which till then could not extort our mind's consent. All those 'changes of heart,' 'awakenings of conscience,' etc., which make new men of so many of us may be classed under this head. The character abruptly rises to another 'level,' and deliberation comes to an immediate end.

"In the *fifth and final type* of decision, the feeling that the evidence is all in, and that reason has balanced the books, may be either present or absent. But in either case we feel, in deciding, as if we ourselves by our own wilful act inclined the beam: in the former case by adding our living effort to the weight of the logical reason which, taken alone, seems powerless to make the act discharge: in the latter by a kind of creative contribution of something instead of a reason which does a reason's work. The slow dead heave of the will that is felt in these instances makes a class of them altogether different subjectively from all the four preceding classes. If examined closely, its chief difference from the former cases appears to be that in these cases the mind at the moment of deciding on the triumphant alternative dropped the other one wholly or nearly out of sight, whereas here both alternatives are steadily held in view, and in the very act of murdering the vanquished possibility the chooser realizes how much in that instant he is making himself lose."

These five methods of deciding are methods which we all use to a greater or less extent. Everyone has probably experienced each of them at some time, yet some people habitually decide by one method and others by another. The man who habitually waits in deciding till all the reasons for and against a line of action are before him belongs to the first class. The man who "flips a copper" whenever anything is to be decided belongs to the second class. The man who is impulsive and who acts "intuitively," but who does not know why he acts so, belongs to the third class. These three classes are known to us all. There is probably no one who decides questions habitually after the manner described in Professor James' fourth and fifth classes.

Of these five methods of decision some are of little significance to the advertiser although of primal significance to the psychologist. The fifth, then, is of no significance to the advertiser except that it is the form which he seeks to obviate. He tries to get the public to dismiss all thought of competing articles. To accomplish this he makes no mention of competitors, but confines his argument to his own commodity.

In the fourth of Professor James' divisions the person, in deciding, passes from the easy and careless to the sober and strenuous mood. This accounts for the fact that certain advertisements may be seen and read frequently with no effect for years, then suddenly this same advertisement becomes all-powerful. This is true in advertising such things as life-insurance, homes, good books, and other forms of merchandise which appeal to the higher nature of man. The reproduced advertisement of Modern Eloquence (No. 1) might not appeal powerfully to readers while they are in a careless and easy mood, but when the mood is changed the same advertisement might be most effective.

The Mood of the Reader

In the third type, which is mainly a form of suggestion, the decision is dependent upon a sudden spontaneity of an emotional nature and leaves but little for the advertiser to do. Women decide after this fashion more frequently than men. Here the advertiser can do most by appealing to the artistic and sentimental natures of the possible customers. The appearance of the advertisement, of the store, or of the salesman is not recognized by the woman as the deciding element, although in reality it is. If a lady were debating the question as to which goods she should order, an appeal to the artistic and sentimental might awaken her emotional nature sufficiently to cause her to decide, and that which awakens the emotion would be likely to be chosen.

A "Woman's Reason"

No. 1.— The effect of this advertisement depends upon the mood of the reader.

Poor Advertising Fairly Successful

The second method of decision is not strictly a reasoning type, but is one which approaches action upon suggestion and hence anything which the advertiser can do to suggest action aids in securing the results which come under this class. This class of persons will not, at the critical moment, search through the back files of magazines to find an advertisement, neither will they exert themselves to find a

No. 2.— A poor advertisement, but one which under certain circumstances might be fairly successful.

store not centrally located if a more convenient one is passed at the critical moment of decision. If I belong to this second of Professor James' classes, and if I am trying to decide which watch I shall buy, I will purchase the one which presents itself to me at the psychological moment, whether the presentation be by advertisement, salesman or store. An extensive advertiser recently said that any kind of advertising would succeed if the advertisements were large and if they appeared frequently enough. This statement is certainly not true but it does find some justification based on the decisions of such persons as are assigned to James' second type. The reproduced advertisement of Pears' Soap (No. 2) is so exceedingly poor that it would be defended by but few. If a man were debating which sort of soap he should purchase and if at the critical moment he should see this advertisement it might possibly induce him to order Pears'. The reproduced advertisement of Cook's Flaked Rice (No. 3) is similar to that of Pears' Soap. If these two advertisements (and others equally poor) were given extensive publicity they would undoubtedly increase the sale of the goods advertised simply because so many persons decide according to Professor James' second class and because so many unimportant questions are decided by us all according to this method. This is no justification of poor advertising, but it helps to explain why poor advertisements are sometimes successful.

Professor James' first method of decision is of the greatest significance to advertisers of all sorts of merchandise, but especially to those who offer goods of a high price and of such a nature that the same person purchases but once or a few times during his life. Among such goods would be included pianos, life-insurance, automobiles and many other advertised articles. Furthermore, the persons who frequently use this first method of deciding are so numerous that it is

No. 3.— A poor advertisement, but one which under certain circumstances might be fairly successful.

essential to appeal to the " reason " of the public in exploiting any kind of merchandise.

The great diversity in individuals and the numerous motives which influence the same individual, added to the apparent complete freedom of the human will, would seem, combined, to make an insuperable obstacle to reasoning with groups of people by any such means as the printed page. Human choice has always been assumed to be unknown, to be the one indeterminable factor in the universe. In spite of all this we have come to see that human action is governed by known laws and that by carefully studying the nature of society and the influences at work prophecies may be made within certain limits which are sufficiently accurate for all practical purposes. Under given political, social and industrial conditions the number and character of crimes remain constant. The suicides distribute themselves in a most remarkable manner, even as to the age, occupation and sex of the person and the manner of committing the crime. The number of marriages each year is more regular than the number of deaths. Famine increases the number of crimes against property and decreases the number of marriages. The wise merchant knows to a certainty from the political, social and industrial condition of the country that there will be increased or decreased demand for individual lines of goods. Despite all the uncertainty of human choice he knows that there are certain conditions which determine the number who will choose his commodity and take the pains to secure it.

Differences in Motives

The advertiser is the diplomat of the commercial and industrial world. It is his duty to know the commodity to be exploited and the public to be reached.

Even though the commodity to be sold may seem very simple, in reality it is not so. The essential thing in every object is the relations which it has and the functions which it fulfills. The presentation of these relationships and functions in a way that will cause the possible purchasers to respond is a task that is not likely to be overestimated.

Suggestion of Evil Consequences to be Avoided

The same goods may be presented in a score of different ways. The goods remain the same, but the manner of presentation meets with marked differences in the response of the public. One presentation may invite suspicion and another confidence. Suspicion is nothing but an exaggerated tendency to call up possible evil consequences, and confidence is an unusual absence of the same tendency. The text and illustration of the advertisement, the make-up, and the reputation of the medium, etc., all unite to increase or decrease this tendency to hesitate and call up possible evil consequences. The advertiser can not be too careful in scrutinizing everything that goes to make up an advertisement to see that nothing is present which would increase the tendency to recall from the past experience evil consequences which have accompanied other actions. The advertising manager of a publication should refuse not only all dishonest advertisements, but also all those which would tend to make readers suspicious, even if such suspicions were ungrounded. A publication which has been taken in the home for years, which has become trusted because of long years of reliable service, is inestimable in its value to the advertiser.

We frequently hesitate to allow time for the suggestion of possible evil consequences, but if such consequences do not suggest themselves in too great a number and with too great vividness, action may follow. Thus persons often respond to advertisements long after they first read them. They could not be induced to respond at once but at a later time they do respond, although there has been no additional ground given for such action. We are all a little suspicious of hasty actions and the older we grow the more suspicious we become. It is frequently wise not to attempt to secure immediate response, for it requires more effort than it would if the public were given a longer time in which to allay their suspicions. Advertisers are frequently surprised by the few responses which they receive at first from their advertisements and by the great response which they secure at a later time, although the first advertisement was in every way as good as the second. There are persons who will answer an advertisement the first time they see it, but there are many others who will not do so. There are some who will answer the first advertisement but will wait a week or so to answer, others will wait till they see the second or third of the series and then answer. The first time they saw the advertisement there was a personal desire for the goods advertised, but the fear of hasty action was enough to restrain action. At a later time such fear is diminished, and the mere fact that the advertisement had begotten a desire upon its first appearance serves to increase the desire upon the second reading of the same or a similar advertisement. Continuous consecutive advertising meets the method of response both of those suggestible creatures who act without hesitation and also of those who are too cautious to respond till after sufficient time has elapsed for all the evil consequences to present themselves.

Suggestion of Substitutes to be Avoided

It was pointed out above that deliberation often occurs because the presentation of one line of action suggests to our minds another similar and incompatible action. This sort of deliberate action, as also that resulting from a suggestion of evil consequences, is common in actions where large interests are at stake. In purchasing an article that costs some hundreds of dollars most persons would deliberate and consider other goods of the same class. Thus in purchasing a piano or an automobile it is to be expected that no one would be satisfied with the presentation of one make but would consider each make in relation to others. Although this is true, yet it is the function of the advertiser to get the public to think of one particular article, and the advertiser should in general make no references to competing goods. The buyer may, indeed, think of such goods as might be purchased, instead of those presented in the advertisement, but the advertiser can not afford to occupy space in furthering this tendency. If the advertisement can be so constructed that it holds the reader's attention to the goods advertised and does not suggest competing goods, it has done much to shorten the period of deliberation and secure decision in favor of the goods advertised. Every slur and every remark intended to weaken the opponent's argument serves to call attention to the goods criticised and thus to divide the reader's attention and so keeps the advertisement from having its due weight.

It is possible to hold two lines of action before us and with both thus attended to, to decide for the one and against the other. Such a decision is made with conscious effort, is unpleasing and is not common. We may debate between two courses of action and hold both clearly in mind for some time, but at the moment of decision one course has usually occupied the mind completely and the other, by dropping from the attention, loses the contest, and action in favor of the object occupying the mind is commenced. What the advertiser must do, therefore, is to help the reader to get rid of the necessity of decision by effort, and he can do this by so presenting his goods that they occupy the attention completely. Under such circumstances decision becomes easy and prompt.

The parts of an advertisement may weaken instead of strengthen each other. One part of the advertisement may offer a substitute which causes us to hesitate about acting upon another part. It is possible to present two articles which seem equally desirable because too little description is given of the articles advertised. In such a case the reader is unable to make up his mind and hesitation and procrastination follow until the initial desire for the goods has vanished. "He who hesitates is lost" is a frequent quotation, but it would be more applicable if we should change it to, "The possible customer who is caused to hesitate is lost." A single advertisement should not present competing goods unless sufficient argument is given to make it possible for the reader to make up his mind and to act at once.

Not only must the advertiser avoid presenting suggestions of evil consequences and possible substitutes for his own commodity but he must use the greatest skill to discover the conception which in any particular case will lead to action. In Professor James' five methods presented above, the most significant thing in the discussion is the following sentence: "The conclusive reason for the decision in these cases usually is the discovery that we can refer the case to a class upon which we are accustomed to act unhesitatingly in a stereotyped way. The moment we hit upon a conception which allows us to apply a principle of action which is a fixed and stable part of our Ego, our state of doubt is at an end."

Recently an attempt was made to discover the conceptions which actually are effective in leading persons to answer advertisements and to purchase advertised goods. Upon this point the statements of several thousand persons were examined. The result was most interesting and instructive. Among the effective motives or conceptions the following were prominent:

1. Reliability of the goods or the firm.
2. The goods supply a present need.
3. Money considerations, e. g., cheapness, investment, chance to win.
4. Labor saving, convenient or useful.
5. Healthful.
6. Stylish.
7. An attractive and frequently repeated advertisement.

Of these seven reasons it will be observed that the second and last should not be included in the reasoning type. In the second the goods were suggested at the time they were needed and the purchase followed without further consideration. In the seventh the purchaser was influenced by the constant suggestion which was offered by the frequently recurrent attractive advertisement.

If the right conception is presented at the right time, the desired action will follow. In the reproduced advertisement of Ivory Soap (No. 4) it is assumed that women purchase the soap and that for many of them, including such as the one shown in the cut, the purity and reliability of the article is the quality of greatest concern. Hence the conception of Ivory Soap as pure and reliable is the one conception above all others which will sell it.

With very many persons it was found that a good investment is the conception which leads to immediate action. Therefore if radiators are presented satisfactorily as a good investment, the question is settled at once and the radiators are purchased. The repro-

No. 4.— Purity as the controlling conception.

duced advertisement of the American Radiator Company (No. 5), appearing in women's magazines, was evidently constructed on this principle.

Very many goods are advertised, and with great success, as being labor-saving, convenient or useful.

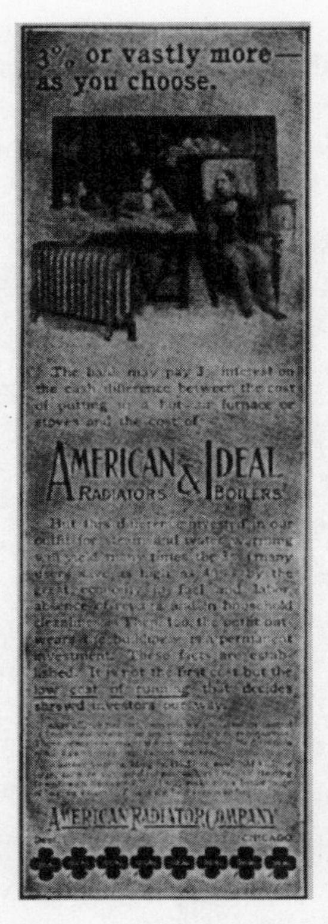

No. 5.—A furnace conceived as a good investment.

The reproduced advertisement of Postum Cereal (No. 6) is open to severe criticism. It should be remembered, however, that there are many persons to whom the conception of health is all powerful. For such this advertisement might be irresistible.

Clothing, diamonds, magazines and hundreds of other things are successfully advertised by emphasis upon the stylishness of the goods: upon the social prestige enjoyed by their possessors.

No. 6.— This series of advertisements assumes the effectiveness of the conception, health.

It is a wise advertiser that can select the conceptions that will fit into the principles of action of the greatest number of possible customers.

IX
HABIT

THE term *habit* has been so frequently confined to a few questionable or bad habits that the broader significance of the term is ordinarily lost.

An Interesting Study

We are all creatures of habit and have some good and some bad ones. It is an interesting study for any one to observe his own actions and thoughts and to see what he does habitually. I tried recently to make such a study of myself, but found that if I should be compelled to record all my habitual actions and thoughts it would keep a stenographer busy all day and a camera would have to be directed toward me for every move I made. I found that I got out of bed in the morning in a way peculiar to myself. I put on my clothes in a stereotyped order. I put my left shoe on first — I always do. I put my coat on by putting on my right sleeve first, and when I tried to reverse the order I found it very difficult. I picked up the morning paper and glanced over the first page; then I turned to the last page and from there looked through the paper from the last to the first page and so ended where I had begun. This is my habitual method of reading the morning paper, although I had not observed the fact till that time.

I put sugar on my breakfast food first and added cream later. The manner in which I arose from the table, put on my hat and left the house was peculiar to myself. My manner of walking was such that my friends, seeing me in the distance, knew me. I walked down town by the same street which I had been going over for years, although there were several other streets equally good and convenient. I addressed my friends in such a manner that they recognized me even when they did not see me. I took up my work and went through it in a regular routine.

The actions as described above were not reasoned out and followed because they were the most rational. I observed my brother's actions at all these points and found that at every point his habits were different from mine. His actions were as reasonable as mine but not more so. Throughout the day I found that the great majority of my actions and thoughts were merely habitual and were performed without conscious desire or deliberation.

Habits and Plasticity

The fact of habit has been a matter of marvel and wonder for centuries, but an explanation of the phenomenon has been left to modern psychology. If I bend a piece of paper and crease it the crease will remain, even if the paper is straightened out again. The paper is plastic, and plasticity means simply that the substance offers some resistance to adopting a new form, but when the new form is once impressed upon it, it retains it. Some effort is required to overcome the plasticity of the paper and to form the crease, but when the crease is once formed the plasticity of the paper preserves the crease.

There is a most intimate relation between our brains and our thoughts. Every time we think there is a slight change taking place in the delicate nerve cells which compose a large part of the brain. Every action among these cells leaves its indelible mark, or "crease," for the nerve substance is plastic. It is easy for the paper to bend where it has been creased and it is likewise easy for action to take place in the brain where it has taken place before. That is why it is so easy to think our old habitual thoughts and why it is so hard to think new thoughts or to perform new movements. When a thought has been thought or an action performed many times, the crease becomes so well established that thinking and acting along that crease are easier than other thoughts or actions, and so these easier ones are said to have become habitual. In a very real sense the thoughts and the actions form the brain, and then when the brain is formed its plasticity is so great that it determines our future thinking and acting.

This is well shown in the case of language. It is ordinarily true that no one ever learns a language after he is twenty-five years old so well that he can speak it without an accent. As far as language is concerned a person seems to be fixed or creased by the time he is twenty-five and he can never get rid of his former habits of speech. Few men ever learn to dress well unless they have acquired the art in their youth. We all know men who have acquired wealth in middle

Learning Late in Life

life and who have tried to be good dressers, but in vain. They go to the best tailors, but something about them betrays their former habits. In all these things we see that we first form our brains, and then when they are once formed (creased) they determine what we shall do and be.

This relationship of the mind to the brain in the formation of habits may be illustrated by the paths in a forest. In the densest forest there are still some paths where you can walk with ease. Some person or some animal walks along in a particular direction and breaks down some of the weeds and briars. Some one else follows, and every time that any one walks in this path it becomes easier. Here the weeds and briars are trampled on and kept out of the way. In all the other places the briars have grown up and made it almost impossible to walk through them.

Every thought we think forms a pathway through our brains and makes it easier for every other similar thought. We think along certain lines and that is the same as saying that we have formed certain pathways of thought through our brains. It is easy now to think these habitual thoughts but to think a new thought is like beating a new path through a forest while to think along the old lines is like following the old paths where advance is easy. A habit in the brain is like a path in a forest. We know how easy it is to take the old path and how hard it is to form a new one. We see how easy it is to think the old thoughts and to do the old things and how difficult the new ones are.

As habits play such a large part in all of our thinking and acting it is important that the advertiser should understand what habits are and how he can make the most of the situation. He should observe the working of the laws of habit in his own life. If he could realize that everything he does leaves on his brain an impression which is to be a determining factor in all his future, he would be extremely careful as to what he thinks and what he does, even in private. The success of the advertiser depends to an exceptionally great degree upon the confidence of the public. If we know that a man acts uniformly in an honest manner we have such confidence in him that we call him an honest man and we believe that he will not break his habit of honesty in the future and we are therefore willing to trust him. Thus, whether we think of single actions as determining our future characters or whether we think of them as determining the estimation in which we shall be held by others, there are no incentives to right actions comparable with the inflexible laws of habit when these laws are fully appreciated.

Good Personal Habits

The advertiser is likely to "get into a rut" in his line of thinking and consequently in his presentation of his commodity before the public. He should see to it that he does not allow his habits gradually but surely to make impossible to him new forms of expression and new lines of thinking and writing. It takes great

Getting Into "Ruts"

and determined effort to overcome an old habit or to form a new one, but the advertiser should in many cases make the necessary effort; otherwise he is doomed to become an "old fogy."

The public, which the advertiser addresses, is subject to the same laws of habit as the advertiser. Each of the potential customers has formed a rut in his thinking and thinks along that particular line or lines. The advertiser must know his customers. He must know their habits of thought, for it is too difficult to attempt to get them to think along new lines. He must present his commodity in such a way that the readers can understand it without being compelled to think a new thought. The advertisement should conform to their habitual modes of thought, and then the customers can read it and understand it with ease.

Your Customers' Habits

Habit gives regularity and persistence to our actions. Some people have formed the habit of looking at the last pages in magazines before they look at the others. Some people look more at the right page than at the left. Some glance first at the top of the page, and if that does not look interesting the page is passed by without a glance at the bottom or middle. The wise advertiser is always alert to detect these habits and to profit by his discovery.

When game is plentiful and hunters few, any marksman may be successful in bagging game. As soon, however, as competition becomes keen only that marksman is successful who understands the habits of the game sought and who plans his method of approach according to the habits of the game. When advertising was more primitive than it is to-day and when competition was less keen, any printer or reporter might have been successful in advertising, but to-day no man can be successful who does not plan his campaign according to the habits of the public which he must reach.

Results Made Permanent

The action of habit gives great value to advertising by making the effect of the advertisement to be not merely transient but permanent. If an advertisement can get persons started to purchasing a particular brand of goods it has done much more than sell the goods in the immediate present; for when people do a thing once it is easier to get them to do it again, and habits are formed by just such repetitions. In the first instance the purchaser may have been induced to act only after much hesitation, but after a few repetitions the act becomes almost automatic and requires little or no deliberation. Habitual acts are always performed without deliberation, and there is a uniformity and a certainty about them which differentiates them from other forms of actions.

One great aim of the advertiser is to induce the public to get the habit of using his particular line of goods. When the habit is once formed it acts as a great drive-wheel and makes further action easy in the same direction. It often takes extensive advertising to get the public into the habit, and the amount of sales may not warrant the expense during the first year, but since a habit formed is a positive asset such campaigns may be profitable.

The advertiser of Pears' soap quoted a great truth when he put this at the head of his advertisement, "How use doth breed a habit." If he could by advertising get persons to using Pears' soap he would get them into the habit of using it, and so the advertisement would be an active agent in inducing the customers to continue to buy the soap even long years after the advertisement had ceased to appear.

Many advertisers work on the theory that as soon as they have got the public into the habit of using their goods they can stop their advertising and the sales will go right on. There is much truth in this but also a great error. It takes so much effort to form the habit that when it is once formed it should be made the most of. This can best be done by continuing the advertising, thus taking advantage of the habit by securing prompt responses and at the same time taking care to preserve the habit.

X
THE HABIT OF READING ADVERTISEMENTS

As was shown in the preceding chapter, we are all creatures of habit. One of the habits which most of us have acquired is that of reading advertisements. The fact that this has become habitual gives it a permanence and regularity similar to that of our other habits. Like other habits, too, we are frequently not conscious of it. I had formed a fixed habit of putting on my right sleeve before the left one, and yet for years I did not know it — would have denied it. People have told me that they never look at the advertising pages of a magazine, when, in fact, they scarcely ever take up a magazine without "glancing" at the advertisements.

One lady told me that she was sure she never paid any attention to advertisements, and yet within an hour after making such a statement she was engaged in a conversation about articles which she knew only from statements appearing in the advertising columns of her periodicals. I observed her reading magazines and found that she seldom slighted the advertisements. Thousands of magazine readers read advertisements more than they are aware.

I asked several professional advertising men as to the number of persons who read advertisements and the time which people in general devote to them. Some of these men assured me that all persons who pick up a magazine look at the advertisements, and that they put in as much time in reading them as they do in reading the body of the magazine. I felt convinced that the advertising men were as wide of the mark as the group first mentioned. It is not possible to find out how much other people read advertisements by observing one's self, by asking personal friends, or by asking those engaged in the business of advertising. To know whether people in general read the advertisements or not it is necessary to watch a large number of persons who are reading magazines, to keep an accurate account of the number who are reading the advertisements and of those who are reading the articles in the body of the magazine. The observation should be made on different classes of persons, in homes, clubs, libraries, on trains — wherever and under whatever conditions people are in the habit of reading publications which contain advertisements.

Some months ago I visited the reading-room of the Chicago Public Library. In this room several hundred men are constantly reading newspapers and magazines — principally magazines. At almost any hour of the day one hundred men may be found there reading magazines. There is a very large number of magazines to choose from, the chairs are comfortable and the light is good. In front of some of the chairs are tables on which the magazine may be rested. There are no conveniences for answering a mail-order advertisement at once, but that might not detract from the reading of such advertisements. Some of the men who read there have but a few minutes to stay, while others are there to spend the day. As I looked over the room to see how many were reading advertisements, it seemed to me that a large part of them were thus engaged.

To know just how many are reading at any particular moment, the following plan of investigation was followed. I began at the first table and, unobserved by the readers, turned my attention to the first man. If he was reading from the body of the magazine, I took what data I wanted from him, jotted them down on my notebook and then turned to his neighbor and took the data from him, etc. A man was reported as reading the advertisements if he was reading them the very first moment I turned my attention to him. In every case this first observation determined the points in question. Thus, if I turned my attention to a man who was looking at the last page of the advertisements, and if the very next moment he turned to the reading matter, he was still reported as reading advertisements. On the other hand, if at my first observation he was just finishing his story in the body of the magazine and if, during the next few minutes, he was engaged in reading advertisements, he was still reported as not reading advertisements. By this system the same results are secured as we should get by taking a snap-shot of the room. We get the exact number who are reading advertisements at any mo-

An Investigation Conducted

ment of time. Where there was a single column of advertisements next to a single column of reading matter at which the subject was looking, it was sometimes impossible to tell what he was reading. In all cases of doubt the man was not counted at all. There were, however, but few such cases.

Percentage Reading Advertisements

I made six visits to the library, going on different days of the week, different seasons of the year and different hours of the day. At each visit I made observations on one hundred men who were reading magazines. Of the first hundred observed eighty-eight were reading from the body of the magazine and twelve were reading advertisements. Of the second hundred six were reading advertisements. Of the third hundred fifteen were reading advertisements. Of the fourth hundred sixteen were reading advertisements. Of the fifth hundred only five were reading advertisements. Of the sixth hundred eleven were reading advertisements. Making a summary of the six hundred magazine readers, I found sixty-five reading advertisements and four hundred and thirty-five reading from the body of the magazine. That is to say, 10½ per cent. of all the men observed were reading advertisements.

At my request a gentleman made similar tests at the same library, and his final results were in remarkable harmony with those given above. Of all the men he observed, exactly ten per cent. were reading advertisements.

The fact that only ten per cent. of the men were reading advertisements at any one point of time is not at all equivalent to saying that only one-tenth of them read — or glanced at — the advertisements. A large part of them turned over the advertising pages, but they turned them hastily and did not stop to read them unless in some way they were particularly interesting. Some of the men were looking at the pictures in the advertising pages; some of them were glancing at the display and reading nothing which was not particularly prominent; others were reading the complete argument of the advertisement. As far as I could tell, most of those who were looking through the advertisements were not engaged in any serious attempt to understand the argument, and were reading in a hasty and indifferent manner. Indeed, it was the exception rather than the rule that any advertisement was read from beginning to end.

Women Interested Most

It is quite certain that the data thus far secured are not sufficient for any generalization as to the exact time or proportion of time which the general public devotes to the advertising columns of periodicals. It is quite generally believed that women read advertisements more than men, but in all the tests referred to above, the data were secured only from men. In the second place, it is true that the regular subscribers to periodicals read them more nearly from cover to cover than readers who drop into a library to read. Magazine readers on a train frequently have but a single copy of a magazine at hand, and as trips are usually somewhat prolonged, the traveler frequently not only reads the text matter but reads many of the advertisements completely. Another element which enters into the question, as here investigated, is found in the fact that among such abundance of periodicals the reader becomes somewhat bewildered, tries to glance through many papers and does not read so carefully as he would ordinarily do under other circumstances. Under these circumstances the data at hand can not show more than certain general tendencies and certain specific facts as to how one class of readers is in the habit of reading the advertisements in magazines under the conditions mentioned above.

The tendency to rush through the advertising pages of magazines, which was so clearly present in the Chicago Public Library, is, I believe, a general tendency. Many people turn every page of the advertising columns of a magazine and read none of the advertisements through. It would not be fair to assume from the data on hand that the average magazine reader spends ten-fold as much time on the text as he does on the advertisements, but it is quite certain that he spends a comparatively short time on the advertisements. If the readers in libraries spend anything like tenfold as much time on the text as on the advertisements, and if there is a general tendency with most readers to rush through or glance at the advertisements, it behooves the advertiser to recognize the actual conditions and to construct his advertisements according to the habits of magazine readers.

If the presentation of his goods is to be seen but a

No. 1.— An illustration that illustrates.

fraction of a second, that fraction must be made to count. The cut used should be not a mere picture but an illustration. The cut should be made to speak for itself and to tell the story so distinctly that at a glance the gist of the advertisement is comprehended. Thus, in the advertisement of Wilson's Outside Venetians (No. 1), reproduced herewith, the illustration shows just how the ware looks and what it

Illustrations Should Illustrate

is good for. Even in the most hasty glance the reader is enabled to get a good idea of the appearance and use of this commodity. If he is interested in such goods at all, this knowledge will often lead him to read the entire advertisement. If he passes the advertisement with a single glance he will still be affected with what he has seen.

The advertisement of the Venus Drawing Pencil,

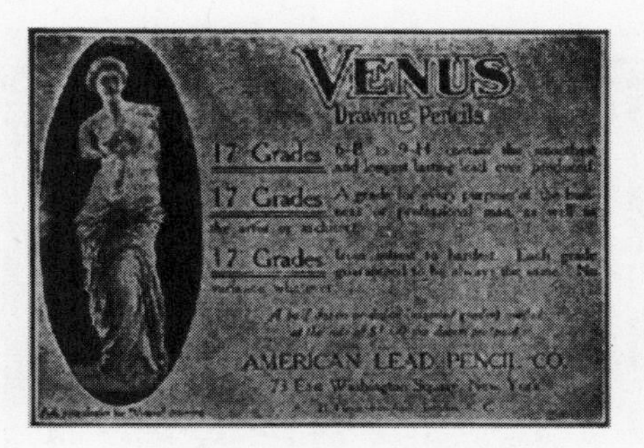

No. 2.— This illustration tells nothing about the goods advertised.

reproduced herewith, (No. 2) has a beautiful picture, but it tells nothing about the goods advertised. I know nothing more about Venus Drawing Pencils after seeing this picture than I did before. Many people look at this picture as they turn the pages of the magazine, and yet they never discover that it has anything to do with pencils. They remember the picture, but do not take the trouble to notice what it is supposed to advertise.

In the advertisement reproduced herewith, the type

display, "Advertising Taught by Mail," (No. 3) gives the gist of the whole matter. Every one who glances at the advertisement understands it. If he sees nothing more than the display of type, he has seen enough to understand what it is all about and to be influenced in favor of the idea there presented. The next time he turns over the pages of a magazine containing this advertisement his attention will be attracted by this familiar display. Every time he sees

No. 3.— The display type gives the gist of the business.

this advertisement the suggestion in favor of it becomes stronger and yet the reader himself may not be conscious of such influence.

In the advertisement reproduced herewith, the type display, "Wanted — Good Neighbors," (No. 4) does not indicate in any way that the advertisement is one of real estate. A person could glance at this advertisement a score of times, but he would know no more about it when he had seen it the last time than he did after he had seen it the first time. It has nothing to say to the casual reader, and would be weakened rather than strengthened by repetition.

About Type Display

The type display should not be merely to attract attention, but must tell a story and tell it quickly. The display type and the picture which merely attract and do not instruct are in many cases worthless, for in attracting attention to themselves they divert the attention

Wanted—
Good Neighbors

Who Value Good Neighbors and a Good Neighborhood About Their Summer Homes.

I want a man—or rather three or four men with $3,000 to $4,000 each, who care as much for a beautiful summer home as I do, to write me and let me tell them of a property I am holding in the most beautiful part of Michigan, for myself and for them. I am not a real estate agent. I am just what I here profess to be, a seeker for a beautiful summer home for myself, with good neighbors. It won't cost you anything to write to me and let me send you some photographs and details. And write now, please, as I do not care to advertise this again. GEORGE MILLS ROGERS, 100 Washington St., Chicago, Ill.

No. 4.—Lacking in indicativeness.

from the thing advertised. The picture and the meaningless headline will interest some people so much that they will stop and read the advertisement through to try to figure out what it all means. But the great majority of the readers will not stop at any particular advertisement, and unless they get something at a glance they get nothing at all. A large number of magazine readers see each advertisement, but only a few of them will stop to read it through. The advertiser must learn to make the best possible use of this casual glance of the multitude. Since many see the display and but few read the argument, an attempt should be made to construct a display that will not merely attract attention to itself, but be so constructed that it will beget interest in the goods advertised.

Few people will admit that they are greatly influenced by advertising. I have discussed the question with many persons, and I have yet to find the first one who believes that he is materially influenced by magazine advertising in the purchases which he makes. One great cause for this personal delusion is found in the habit which they have formed of glancing through the advertising pages. They turn the pages rapidly and the individual advertisement makes so little impression that it is not remembered by them as having been seen at all.

Unrecognized Value of Advertisements

To say that the advertisement is forgotten is not equivalent to saying that it has not made a lasting impression. If I should glance at the same advertisement in different magazines for each month for a number of years, it is quite possible that these single glances would be forgotten. I might not remember ever having seen an advertisement, and yet my familiarity with the goods advertised might seem so great that I should believe that some of my acquaintances had recommended them to me or that I had used the goods years before.

The following instance, which was also referred to in the chapter on Suggestion, illustrates this point perfectly. For years I have seen the advertisements of a certain tailor. Recently I entered his shop and ordered a suit of clothes. It so happened that the proprietor, who was conducting a vigorous advertising campaign, waited on me himself. As he took my order he asked me whether he had been recommended to me. I promptly replied that he had. I then began to try to recall who had recommended him, but found that I could not recall any such recommendation. I had seen his advertisement so often that I had forgotten the particular advertisements, but had retained the information which they had imparted. I had evidently confused the source of my information, for I fully believed that I had heard from some of my friends that this particular tailor was especially trustworthy. If he had asked me whether I had been influenced by his advertisements or not, I might have answered that they had had nothing to do with it, although in fact they were the only source of my information about him and evidently were entirely responsible for the sale.

The oftener we see an advertisement, the fewer are the chances that we will remember where we saw it, but the greater becomes our feeling of familiarity with the goods advertised. As soon as we become

Familiarity With the Goods

familiar with the goods in this way and unmindful of the source of the familiarity, we are likely to be subject to this delusion of supposing that we have heard our friends recommend the goods. Most people still are prejudiced against advertisements, and would not purchase the goods if they realized that their only source of information about the firm and about the goods was the advertisement; but as soon as they forget the source of the information they are perfectly willing to buy the goods, although they would repudiate the statement that they had been influenced by the advertisements. If a merchant should ask his customers whether they had been influenced largely by his advertisements or not, he would certainly receive a very discouraging report, and would be inclined to give up his advertisements as worthless, when, in fact, nothing but his advertisements had induced them to come to his store.

The habit which the public has formed of reading advertisements so hastily makes it difficult for the advertisement writer to construct his advertisements to meet the emergency of the case; it makes it difficult for the merchant to discover the direct results of his advertising campaign, and, on the other hand, it makes the right sort of advertising peculiarly effective, by making the reader more susceptible to confusion as to the source of his information.

XI
THE LAWS OF PROGRESSIVE THINKING

Four Processes of Progressive Thinking

In acquiring simple acts of skill we all use in the main the "try, try again" method. This is technically known as the "trial and error" method. We simply keep trying till we happen to hit it right, and then we imitate our successes till finally the skill is acquired. The first correct response may have been reflex, instinctive or merely accidental. When, however, we attempt to develop acts of skill or ideas in advance of our fellows this simple method of trial and error does not suffice. It is of course true that most of the actions of all of us and all the acts of many of us are not progressive in the sense here intended. By progressive thinking we mean the conception of new ideas, the invention of new methods of doing work, the construction of a new policy or a new instrument or something of a kindred nature. For such thinking the essential mental process involves nothing totally different from ordinary thinking, but it involves the ordinary processes in a more complete and efficient form. The processes referred to are the following four: observation, classification, inference and application. The laws of progressive thinking are derived from these processes and are nothing more than a demand for the complete carrying out of these four processes. The thinking of the advertiser does not differ from that of others; and in what follows the discussion will be confined to the advertiser and his problems, inasmuch as such a concrete problem seems more definite than a general discussion.

Observation

Observation is logically the first step. All advertisers have eyes, but they do not all use them equally well. Observation should begin at home. The advertiser should analyze his own response to advertisements, but unfortunately he is likely to become so prejudiced or hardened to advertisements that his own judgment must be taken with great caution. How does this advertisement or this part of the advertisement affect me? How does it affect my wife, my mother, my sister? How does it affect the persons who ride on the train with me or who pass by the billboards with me? This is the territory which is so near at home that we disregard it. Such observations must, of course, be supplemented by tests carried on by means of keying the advertisement, by consulting the sales department, etc.

None of us are ideal observers. We can't tell just how certain advertisements affect us or what element of the advertisement is the most effective. We do not observe accurately how advertisements affect those about us. We see only those things which we have learned to see or which have been pointed out to us. We are not skillful in discovering new methods of securing new data and so our observations are neither so accurate nor so extensive as they should be.

The advertiser has an extensive field of observation

and but little direction as to the best method. He must observe his goods in order to know the possible qualities which may be presented with greatest force. He must observe the public to which he is to make his appeal. He must be a practical psychologist. He must also be an advertising expert according to the narrow and fallacious use of that term. In the past the advertiser has not been required to know his commodity or his public, but he has felt satisfied if he was an expert in the construction of advertisements, the choice of mediums, the keying of advertisements and similar strictly technical accomplishments. The observations are not complete unless they include these three fields, i. e., the goods, the public and the advertisements.

Classification

The second step in the method, logically speaking, is that of classification. The observations must be classified. The scattered data must be brought together before they can be utilized. Great skill is necessary to make the right classifications. In any large office care must be used in filing away material to see that the general heads are not only correct but that they are the most usable ones. Likewise in filing away our observations, in getting them into shape so that we can use them, the greatest care is necessary in choosing the right heads and in getting all the data under their appropriate general heads. All the data must be analyzed and classified and reclassified, for new observations require new classifications, so that the classification is never complete and the generalizations based on the classifications are continually increasing. For instance, every advertiser has a certain amount of data concerning the effectiveness of advertisements without illustrations in publications in which the text matter is largely illustrated. But how many advertisers have grouped this data and formed any general statement concerning it?

The process of classification involves that of analysis, and the difficulty of forming new analyses is much greater than would be supposed by those who have not studied the process. In order that new classifications may be made the data must be worked over and thought of in all the possible relations. The man who makes the best use of his knowledge is the one who has it best analyzed and classified.

Inference

Advertisers have sent me two different advertisements which were carefully keyed, one of which was successful and the other one unsuccessful. In some cases the advertisements are very similar and the differences at first sight seem non-essential, yet the differences are great enough to secure success in one case and failure in another. Under some circumstances it might be practically impossible to deduce the cause of the differences. Recently an advertiser sent me two such advertisements. One had been unsuccessful and the other had been extremely successful. The illustrations were very similar and the arguments were largely identical throughout. The two had been run in the same sizes and in the same and also in different publications. It seemed quite evident that the difference must lie in the advertisements themselves and not in any extraneous matter.

I think that I was correct in inferring that the difference lay in the display of the illustration and text matter, but not in the quality of either of them. In the unsuccessful advertisement there was no resting place for the eye and no point or line of orientation. (The line of orientation is the line which the eye follows in observing an illustration.) In the successful advertisement the eye rested naturally at the point from which the advertisement looked the most artistic and from which the content of the advertisement could best be understood. Furthermore, the line of orientation was such that the eye naturally followed the order which made the argument and display mutually strengthening, and so the eye rested, at the conclusion, at the point which was most inducive to immediate action. Any trained artist or even any one who had studied the theory which underlies artistic productions, might very naturally have looked for this resting place for the eye or for the appropriate place for the line of orientation, but unless these features were taken into consideration the wrong conclusion would have been drawn as to the cause of success or failure in the case of these two advertisements.

The fourth step in the mental process of the progressive advertiser is that of applying the deductions drawn from the former experience. The laws concerning the force called electricity are known to thousands, but it takes an Edison or a Marconi to make a new application of these same laws. If Edison and Marconi had not a comprehensive grasp of these laws they would not be inventors. Others have as good a knowledge of all the phenomena connected with electricity as they and yet are unable to make a practical use of their knowledge. Science can formulate the laws of the phenomena as far as they have been discovered and applied, but it can not lay down rules or suggest infallible methods for further discoveries and inventions. This does not minimize the value of science but it emphasizes the need of originality and ingenuity in the man who strives to lead his profession and to invent new methods and to make new applications of those he has learned.

Application

Certain keen students of advertising have prophesied but little benefit to advertising from the science of psychology, because a science can not lay down rules for things which are not yet discovered. This criticism has weight with any who should be so foolish as to suppose that every accomplished student of the human mind would of necessity be a successful advertiser. To suppose that a great psychologist would of necessity be a successful innovator in advertising is just as sane as to suppose that every one who understands electricity as well as Edison would have as great a record as he at the patent office. If Edison had known nothing of the science of physics, it is quite certain that he never would have been heard from. Science does not produce inventors but it is of great assistance to a genius and may cause him to become a great discoverer. Psychology is of assistance to every advertiser in helping him to observe widely and accurately, in teaching him how to classify or group his observations systematically: it should help him in drawing the correct conclusions from his classified experience. If psychology could do no more it would be of inestimable value, but as applications or new discoveries depend so largely on the formation of correct deductions and hypotheses, psychology may even be of benefit in this last and most difficult step in the mental process of the innovator.

The Method Further Illustrated

The most successful advertisers are those who observe most widely and accurately, who classify their observations and group them in the most usable form, who then think most keenly about these classified observations so as to draw the most helpful conclusions, and lastly who have the greatest ability in utilizing these deductions in their advertising campaigns. They are the active men, those who are seeking better methods of observation and of classification and who are never content with their past deductions or their applications. To show what I mean at this point I will illustrate from methods employed by one of the leading advertisers of America.

In observing the effect which advertisements produce upon a community it is much easier to learn which advertisements are effective than what it is in the particular advertisements which makes them interesting. Mr. B., as an aid in making observations at this latter point, secured several thousands of letters from readers of issues of the magazine of which he was the advertising manager. In these letters the writers told which advertisements they were the most interested in and what it was in each particular advertisement which interested them. Mr. B. could have turned to the pages of his magazine and have made a personal observation as to the way the different advertisements affected him and what it was in any particular advertisement which interested him most, but by the method described he multiplied his observations a thousand fold, and all within the commodity with which he has to deal. When he had read over the letters he had the data before him but it was in chaotic and worthless condition. The next step was to bring order out of chaos. It was easy to tabulate the results and find out how many were especially interested in each particular advertisement. But when it came to classifying the reasons — and often women's reasons at that — for being interested in each advertisement, the task proved itself to be one of great difficulty.

The data were turned over to me for such classification, and though this is not the place to give in full the general heads and the sub-heads under which the classification was finally made, it may be interesting to know that the reasons for advertisements' proving interesting were in the order of their frequency: first, reliability; second, financial consideration; third, the construction of the advertisement; and fourth, the present need of the reader. Thus of the letters received one month, 607 affirmed that they were most interested in their chosen advertisement because they believed that the firm or the medium or the goods were strictly reliable. In some cases they had tried the goods advertised; in some they had dealt with the firm; in some they noticed the testimonials or the prizes taken, etc. In the same month 508 were particularly interested because of money considerations. Some because they could get the goods advertised more cheaply than elsewhere; some because the advertisements offered a chance to get something for service instead of for cash, etc., etc. In the same month 418 were most interested in the construction of the advertisement. Some were most interested, for instance, in the Nestle's Food advertisement, because it was very artistic and was run in colors. In the same month 408 were most interested in a particular advertisement because it presented goods which they needed at that particular time. To recapitulate the results: 607 for reliability, 508 for money considerations, 418 for the construction of the advertisement, and 408 because of the present need.

It is not necessary to say that from the classifications of these data certain conclusions have been drawn and that attempts are being made to apply the conclusions to the planning of advertising campaigns. These experimental applications will furnish new data; these will in turn be classified, new conclusions deduced and further attempts at practical application will follow. In this way we have an endless chain of observation, classification, inference and application. This method is applicable not only to writing advertisements but to every detail of the profession. Indeed it is the method of progressive thinking in every line of human endeavor. The four steps are not fully differentiated in our actual experience but are presented here as distinct for the sake of clearness.

XII
ATTENTION VALUE OF SMALL AND OF LARGE SPACES

THERE are certain things which seem to force themselves upon us whether we will or not. We seem to be compelled to attend to them by some mysterious instinctive tendency of our nervous organization. Thus moving objects, sudden contrasts, large objects, etc., seem to catch our attention with irresistible force. Again there are certain conditions which favor attention and others which hinder it. Among the conditions favoring attention the following is, for the advertiser, of special significance. *The power of any object to compel attention depends upon the absence of counter attraction.* In another discussion of the subject of Attention appeared the following paragraph (Theory of Advertising, page 9): "Other things being equal, the probabilities that any particular thing will catch our attention are in proportion to the absence of competing attractions. This may be demonstrated in a specific case as follows: I had a card of convenient size and on it were four letters. This card was exposed to view for one twenty-fifth of a second, and in that time all the four letters were read by the observers. I then added four other letters and exposed the card one twenty-fifth of a second as before. The observers could read but four of the letters

A Fundamental Law of Attention

as in the previous trial but in this exposure there was no certainty that any particular letter would be read. I then added four more letters to the card and exposed the letters as in the previous trials. The observers were still able to read but four letters. That is to say, up to a certain point all could be seen. When the number of objects (i. e., letters) was doubled, the chances that any particular object would be seen was reduced fifty per cent. When the number of objects was increased threefold, the chances of any particular object's being seen were reduced to thirty-three per cent. If I should place any particular four letters on the right and also the same letters on the left hand page of any magazine and have nothing else on the page, it is safe to say that the letters would be seen, with more or less attention, in one or both cases by every one who turns over the pages of the magazine. This follows because at the ordinary reading distance the field of even comparatively distinct vision is smaller than a single page of ordinary magazine size, and as one turns the pages the attention is ordinarily not wider than the page, and therefore the letters have no rivals and would of necessity fill or occupy the attention for an instant of time, or until the page was turned over. If one hundred of these letters are placed on each of the pages the chances that any particular letter will be seen are greatly reduced. This seems to indicate that, other things being equal, the full-page advertisement is the 'sure-to-be-seen' advertisement and that the size of an advertisement determines the number of chances it has of being seen."

Even a casual reader of advertisements is aware of the fact that full-page advertisements attract his attention more than smaller advertisements. Every advertiser knows that if he should occupy full pages he would secure more attention than if he should occupy quarter pages, yet one of the most perplexing questions which any advertiser has to deal with is the adequate amount of space for any particular advertisement or for any particular advertising campaign. The question is not as to the superiority of full pages in comparison with smaller spaces. All feel sure that any advertisement would be more valuable if it occupied a full page than if it occupied only half of it. But the real question is whether it is twice as valuable, for it costs practically twice as much. A quarter-page announcement is valuable but a half-page is worth more — is it worth twice as much? It is of course conceded that some advertisements are unprofitable regardless of the space occupied, and that others are profitable when filling various amounts of space. It is also conceded that certain advertisements require a large space and that others are profitable as an inch advertisement but would be unprofitable if inflated to occupy a full page.

There are exceptions and special cases but the question can be intelligently stated as follows: Of all the advertisements being run in current advertising which is the more profitable, in proportion to the space occupied, the large or the small advertisements? Since profitableness is a very broad term and depends upon many conditions, we will for the present confine ourselves to one of the characteristics of a profitable advertisement, i. e., its attention value.

The quotation presented above was deduced from a theoretical study of attention, before opportunity had been offered to verify it by means of experiments with advertisements. To investigate the question the following tests were made: I handed each of the forty students in my class a copy of the current issue of the Century Magazine. I then asked them to take the magazines and look them through, just as they ordinarily do, but not to read any poetry or long articles. Some of them put in all their time reading advertisements; some glanced through the advertisements, read over the table of contents and looked over the reading matter; a few failed even to look at the advertisements. At the end of ten minutes, I surprised them by asking them to lay aside the magazines and write down all they could remember about each of the advertisements they had seen. I sent the same magazines to other persons in other parts of the country and had them use the magazines in the same way in which I had used them. In this way tests were made with over five hundred persons mostly between the ages of ten and thirty.

An Investigation

These results were carefully tabulated as to the exact number of persons who mentioned each individual advertisement. We then got together all references to each particular advertisement and so could compare the different advertisements, not only as to the fact of bare remembrance, but also as to the amount of information which each had furnished, the desire it had created to secure the goods, etc. At the present time we shall consider all advertisements mainly from the standard of attracting attention sufficiently to be recalled by those who saw them.

Out of the ninety-one full-page advertisements, sixty-four of them are advertisements of books and periodicals, while of the half-page, quarter-page and small advertisements there is a total of about five pages devoted to books and periodicals. To compare the full-page advertisements with the other advertisements in this particular magazine would be to compare advertisements of books and periodicals with advertisements of other classes of goods. To obviate this difficulty, we shall divide all advertisements into two classes: (1) Those of goods other than books and periodicals; (2) Those of books and periodicals.

The twenty-seven full-page advertisements of goods other than books or periodicals were remembered (mentioned in the reports of the five hundred persons tested) 530 times, which is an average of approximately 20 for each advertisement. The sixty-four full-page advertisements of books and periodicals were remembered 606 times, which is an average of 9 times for each advertisement.

The thirty-nine half-page advertisements of goods

other than books or periodicals were mentioned 358 times, which is an average of 9 times for each advertisement.

The sixty-seven quarter-page advertisements, other than those of books or periodicals, were mentioned 223 times, which is an average of 3 for each advertisement. The three quarter-page advertisements of books and magazines were mentioned only twice which is an average of less than 1 for each advertisement.

As less than a single quarter-page of small advertisements was of books and periodicals, it is useless to consider such advertisements separately. There are ninety-eight small advertisements, and these were mentioned but 65 times which is an average of much less than 1 for each advertisement.

The inefficiency of the small advertisement is made more striking when we consider that for all advertisements other than for those of books and periodicals a full page was mentioned approximately 20 times, a half-page 9 times, a quarter-page 3 times, and a small advertisement less than a single time. As is shown in the following table of all advertisements other than those of books and periodicals, a quarter-page advertisement was mentioned 30% oftener than a quarter page of small advertisements; a half-page advertisement was mentioned 80% oftener than a half page of small advertisements; and a full-page of advertisements was mentioned 90% oftener than a full page of small advertisements.

The tabulated results for all advertisements other than of books and periodicals are as follows:

Size of Advertisement. ☞	Full-page.	Half-page.	Quarter-page.	Small.
Number of advertisements.............	27	39	67	98
Pages occupied........................	27	18½	16¾	6
Total number out of 500 persons who mentioned them.....................	530	358	223	65
Average number of mentions for each advertisement	$19\frac{17}{27}$	$9\frac{7}{39}$	3	$\frac{65}{98}$
Average number of mentions for each page occupied	$19\frac{17}{27}$	$18\frac{14}{39}$	13	10

When we consider the advertisements for books and periodicals, the differences are enormous. A half-page advertisement was noticed 50% oftener than two quarter-page advertisements, and a full-page advertisement was mentioned 250% oftener than four quarter-page advertisements.

The tabulated results for advertisements of books and periodicals are as follows:

Size of Advertisement. ☞	Full-page.	Half-page.	Quarter-page.	Small.
Number of advertisements.............	64	8	3	Less than a single quarter-page of small advertisements of books and periodicals.
Pages occupied........................	64	4	¾	
Total number out of 500 persons who mentioned them.....................	606	16	2	
Average number of mentions for each advertisement	$9\frac{15}{32}$	2	$\frac{2}{3}$	
Average number of mentions for each page occupied.....................	$9\frac{15}{32}$	4	$2\frac{2}{3}$	

Numerical Results Not Sufficiently Explicit

An advertisement was regarded as "remembered" if it was mentioned at all. In some instances the illustration alone was remembered and the person mentioning it was unable to tell what advertisement the illustration was used with. In a few instances the illustration of one brand of goods was interpreted as an advertisement of the competing

a Room. Seward School Minneapolis.
May. 13, 1902

When looking through this magazine I found one advertisement which attracted my attention. This one was on page 60, was one of two little boys represented as being out in the winter cold How jolly they look and what an expression they have in their face as if there was no winter to them These two "chaps" surely will need Packer's Tar Soap, for their chapped hands after snow-balling. This advertisement attracts my attention because of the picture and also because of the advertisement itself.

Esther Hedlund.

No. 1.— This report indicates the educational value of this advertisement.

brand. On the other hand the results were frequently astounding in their revelation of the effectiveness of the advertisements in imparting the essential information and creating a desire for the goods. The above cut (No. 1), is a reproduction of the report of one of the pupils in Minneapolis, made after she had looked through the magazine for ten minutes without the knowledge that she would be called upon to report on what she had read. The advertisement described by this pupil was mentioned more than any other and is reproduced herewith as No. 2.

No. 2.— A full page advertisement possessing great attention value.

An Investigation With Fifty Adults

Soon after the completion of the investigation described above a supplementary investigation was devised to see whether similar results would be secured from a more diversified list of advertisements and from the class of persons for whom the advertisements were especially written. We took the binding wires out of a large number of magazines and thus were able to make a collection of advertising pages without tearing the margins of the leaves. We made use of magazines of different years and of different kinds, but all used were of uniform magazine size. From these leaves we chose one hundred pages of advertisements, being careful to choose as many different styles of advertisements as possible. We had in these pages advertisements of almost everything which has been advertised in magazines of recent years. We had all the different styles of display, of type and illustration, of colored cuts and tinted paper, etc. We had these hundred pages bound up with the body of a current magazine, and the whole thing looked like any ordinary magazine. Indeed, no one suspected that it was " made up " as he looked at it.

This specially prepared magazine was handed to fifty adults. A large part of them were heads of families, readers of magazines, and purchasers of the goods advertised. Thirty-three of them were women and seventeen men. Some of them lived in a city and some in a country town. As we had tried to choose all the different kinds of advertisements possible, so we tried to get all kinds and conditions of people for subjects. With three exceptions, the subjects knew nothing of the nature of the experiment. Some of them knew that it was for experimental purposes, but some of them merely took the magazine and looked it through, supposing that it was the latest magazine. Each one was requested to look through the magazine and, in every case tabulated, all the hundred pages of advertisements were turned. Some of the subjects turned the pages rapidly and got through in three minutes, others were thirty minutes in getting through. The average time for the fifty subjects was a little over ten minutes.

As soon as each subject had completely looked through the magazine it was taken away from him and he was asked to "mention" all the advertisements which he had seen, and to tell all about each of them. What he said was written down, and then the subject was given the magazine again and asked to look it through and indicate each advertisement which he recognized as one which he had seen but had forgotten to mention.

There was very great diversity in individuals in their ability to mention the advertisements which they had just seen. Some of them mentioned as high as thirty different advertisements; one man was unable to mention a single advertisement which he had seen, although all the one hundred pages of advertisements had been before his eyes but a moment before.

Diversity Among Observers

There was also great diversity in subjects in their ability to recognize the advertisements when they looked through the magazine the second time. Some of them recognized as high as one hundred advertisements when looking through the second time and were surprised that they had forgotten to mention them. Others, in looking through the second time, were surprised to see how unfamiliar the magazine looked. One subject, who mentioned but three advertisements, could recognize only three others. He had no recollection of having seen any of the others. This would seem to indicate that certain persons may turn over the advertising pages of a magazine and yet hardly see the advertisements at all.

As in the previous investigations, we divided all advertisements into two classes: (1) advertisements of goods other than books and periodicals and called, therefore, miscellaneous advertisements; (2) advertisements of books and periodicals.

The forty-three pages of full-page miscellaneous advertisements were mentioned 281 times and recognized 544 times. That is, each of these advertisements was mentioned on an average of $6\ ^{23}/_{43}$ times and recognized on an average of $12\ ^{28}/_{43}$ times in addition.

The thirty-one full-page advertisements of books and periodicals were mentioned 85 times by the fifty subjects, which is an average of $2\ ^{23}/_{31}$ times for each advertisement. The thirty-one full-pages were recognized (upon looking through the magazine a second time) 276 times by the fifty subjects, in addition to the "mentions." Each of these advertisements was thus recognized on an average almost 9 times.

The fifteen half-page advertisements of miscellaneous advertisements were mentioned 41 times, which is an average of $2\ ^{11}/_{15}$ times for each. The fifteen advertisements were recognized 118 times in addition, which is an average of $7\ ^{13}/_{15}$ times for each one.

There are but four half-page advertisements of books and periodicals, and only one of them was mentioned by any of the fifty, and that but once. That gives an average of ¼ mention for each advertisement. They were recognized by 24, which is an average of 6 for each advertisement.

The thirty-six quarter-page miscellaneous advertisements were mentioned 39 times, which is an average of $1\ ^{1}/_{12}$ times for each advertisement. They were recognized 122 times, which is an average of $3\ ^{7}/_{18}$ times for each. There are six quarter-page advertisements of books and periodicals. These six were mentioned only 3 times, which is an average of ½ for each advertisement.

The ninety-three small miscellaneous advertisements were mentioned 14 times, which makes an average of $^{14}/_{93}$. They were recognized 34 times, which is an average of $^{34}/_{93}$ for each advertisement. Of the small advertisements only seven were of books and periodicals; these seven were mentioned once, which is an average of $^{1}/_{7}$ for each. The seven were recognized only twice, or on the average of $^{2}/_{7}$.

The following tabulations will make clear the results secured from fifty adults:

Tabulated results for all miscellaneous advertisements secured from fifty adults as follows:

Size of Advertisement. ☞	Full-page.	Half-page.	Quarter-page.	Small.
Number of Advertisements	43	15	36	93
Pages occupied	43	$7\frac{1}{2}$	9	$5\frac{1}{2}$
Total number of mentions	281	41	39	14
Average number of mentions for each advertisement	$6\frac{23}{43}$	$2\frac{11}{15}$	$1\frac{1}{12}$	$\frac{14}{93}$
Average number of mentions for each page occupied	$6\frac{23}{43}$	$5\frac{7}{15}$	$4\frac{1}{3}$	$2\frac{6}{11}$
Total (additional) number of recognitions	544	118	122	34
Average number of recognitions for each advertisement	$12\frac{28}{43}$	$7\frac{13}{15}$	$3\frac{7}{18}$	$\frac{34}{93}$
Average number of recognitions for each page occupied	$12\frac{28}{43}$	$15\frac{11}{15}$	$13\frac{5}{9}$	$6\frac{2}{11}$

Tabulated results for all advertisements of books and periodicals secured from fifty adults as follows:

Size of Advertisements. ☞	Full-page.	Half-page.	Quarter-page.	Small.
Number of Advertisements	31	4	6	7
Pages occupied	31	2	$1\frac{1}{2}$	$\frac{1}{2}$
Total number who mentioned them	85	1	3	1
Average number of mentions for each advertisement	$2\frac{23}{31}$	$\frac{1}{4}$	$\frac{1}{2}$	$\frac{1}{7}$
Average number of mentions for each page occupied	$2\frac{23}{31}$	$\frac{1}{2}$	2	1
Total (additional) number of recognitions	276	24	11	2
Average number of recognitions for each advertisement	$8\frac{28}{31}$	6	$1\frac{5}{6}$	$\frac{2}{7}$
Average number of recognitions for each page occupied	$8\frac{28}{31}$	12	$7\frac{1}{3}$	4

As is shown by the foregoing, for all kinds of advertisements, with but one exception, a full-page advertisement was mentioned oftener than two half-page advertisements; two half-page advertisements were mentioned oftener than four quarter-page advertisements, and four quarter-page advertisements were mentioned oftener than a full page of small advertisements. The exception referred to is the half-page advertisements of books which fell below all other-sized advertisements, but as the number of "recognized" is very large, the apparent exception should not be emphasized.

Viewing the Ads. Twice

Although an advertisement had not impressed the reader sufficiently to enable him to mention it after he had closed the magazine, yet it may have made such an impression on him that he could recall it if a need or something else should arise to suggest it to his mind. Thus, to find out how many of the advertisements had made any appreciable impression, we had each subject see how many of the advertisements in the magazine he could recognize a few minutes after he had looked through it for the first time. The results given above indicate that a quarter-page advertisement was recognized oftener than a quarter page of small advertisements; that a half-page advertisement was recognized oftener than two quarter-page advertisements; but that the full-page advertisements in three instances were recognized less often proportionately than smaller advertisements, i. e., half-page and quarter-page miscellaneous advertisements and half-page advertisements of books and periodicals.

These three exceptional instances are of no significance inasmuch as the full-page advertisements had been previously mentioned and therefore had been excluded from those that could be merely recognized.

The report given by each subject was carefully analyzed to see how many times each advertisement impressed a subject sufficiently so that he would know at least what general class of goods the advertisement represented. Upon comparing the reports upon the different advertisements at this point, it was found that the subject knew what class of goods the full-page advertisement represented much better than what the half-page represented; that the half-page was better than the quarter-page, and that the quarter-page was better than the small advertisement.

Relative Values Shown

Results were then compiled as to the comparative values of the different-sized advertisements in impressing upon the subjects the individual brand or name of the goods advertised. It was found that this information was imparted much better by the larger advertisements. In a similar way, results were compiled as to the name and address of the firm, the price of the goods offered and the line of argument presented by the advertiser. In all of these cases it was found that the full-page advertisement was more than twice as effective as a half-page advertisement; a half-page was more than twice as effective as a quarter-page, and a quarter-page was more effective than a quarter page of small advertisements.

The full-page advertisements which were mentioned by the greatest number of subjects were Ivory Soap

No. 3.— This full page advertisement attracts attention. Does it sell soap?

(mentioned 24 times and reproduced herewith as No. 3), In-er-Seal (mentioned 23 times) and Pears' Soap (mentioned 20 times, reproduced herewith as No. 4). Of the 24 persons who mentioned Ivory Soap (No. 3) but sixteen knew that it was an advertisement of soap at all, and only fourteen knew that it was an advertisement of Ivory Soap. Of the twenty-three persons who mentioned In-er-Seal, only sixteen knew that it referred to biscuits, while but nine knew that it was an advertisement of In-er-Seal goods. The advertisement in question is the familiar one of a boy in a raincoat putting packages of In-er-Seal in a cupboard. Of

No. 4.—Full page reproduction effective as mere display advertising.

the twenty persons who mentioned Pears' Soap (No. 4), every one of them knew that it was an advertisement of Pears' Soap. Only five of the full-page advertisements were mentioned by none of the fifty subjects. These five were of the New York Central Railroad (No. 5), Egyptian Deities Cigarettes, Waltham Watches (No. 6), Equitable Life Insurance Company and the Lyman D. Morse Advertising Agency. There

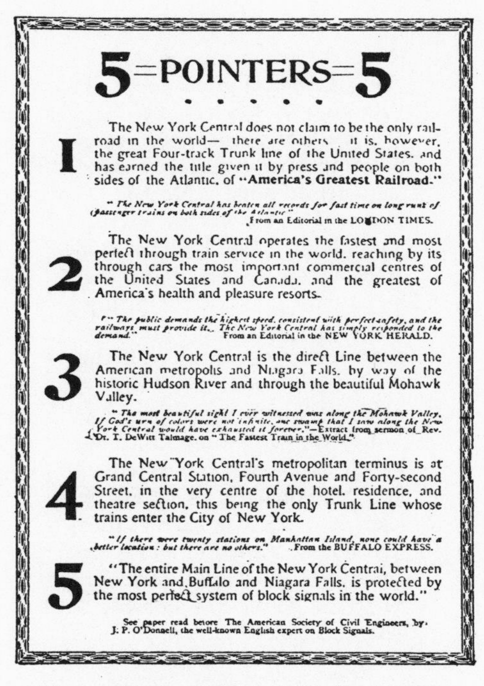

No. 5.— Weak attention value in any size.

were very many half-page, quarter-page and small advertisements which were mentioned and recognized by none of the fifty persons tested.

The results indicated a very great difference between

individual advertisements which filled the same space.

Quality First; Size Next

Quality is more important than quantity. Certain styles of advertisements (depending upon the goods advertised as well as on other things) are effective in any space,

Nobody wants a poor watch. We all want a good one. The *American Waltham Watch Company* has made it possible for everybody to own a perfect watch at a moderate price. No one need go to Europe for a watch nowadays. The best are made in Waltham, Mass., right here in America. The Company particularly recommends the movements engraved with the trade-mark *"Riverside"* or *"Royal"* (made in various sizes), which cost about one-third as much as foreign movements of the same quality. All retail jewelers have them or can get them. Do not be misled or persuaded into paying a larger price for a watch no better and probably not so good as a *Waltham*.

No. 6.—An advertisement possessing but little attention value.

and others are comparatively worthless, even if filling a full page. An advertiser should certainly give more heed to the quality of his advertisement than to its size, yet the size is an important element.

In the case of these one hundred pages of typical advertisements, the size of the advertisements affected their value materially. In the number of times the advertisement was mentioned from memory, in the number of times it was recognized when the magazine was looked at for the second time, and in the number of times that the advertisement conveyed definite information as to the general class of goods advertised, the specific name or brand of the goods, the name of the firm, the address of the firm, the price of the goods and the argument presented in favor of the goods — in all of these points (disregarding the exception mentioned above) the full-page advertisement was more than twice as effective as the half-page; the half-page was more than twice as effective as the quarter-page; the quarter-page was more effective than a quarter page of small advertisements. In other words, at all points considered in the two investigations described above, the value of an advertisement increases as the size of the advertisement increases, and the increase of value is greater than the increase in the amount of space filled.

XIII
THE MORTALITY RATE OF ADVERTISERS

In the preceding chapter it was shown that the larger advertisements attract the attention much more than the smaller ones. The larger ones also offer more opportunity for relevant text and appropriate illustrations. The larger advertisements are best for imparting the desired information and for making a lasting impression on the possible customers. Many business men, however, believe that the small advertisement is safer than the larger one and that the larger spaces are luxuries reserved for those who are able to incur losses without serious consequences.

If the users of large spaces are reckless and the users of small spaces cautious and conservative, we should naturally suppose that the more conservative firms would be the ones which would stay in business longest and which might be looked for in each successive year in the advertising pages of certain magazines. There is a tradition that the users of advertising space are, as a whole, rather ephemeral, that they are in the magazines to-day and to-morrow have ceased to exist. There are, on the other hand, persons with perfect faith in advertising who believe that all a firm has to do is to advertise and its success is assured.

This chapter presents the results of extensive investigations carried on to ascertain more definitely the stability of advertisers and to discover which sizes of advertisements seem to be the safest and most profitable.

Data were secured from all firms located west of Buffalo and advertising in the Ladies' Home Journal for a period of eight years. All firms were grouped together which had appeared in this magazine but one of these years, all which had appeared two of the years, all which had appeared three of the years, etc., up to and including all of the firms which had appeared the eight years under consideration. After a careful analysis had been made the following significant results were secured:

The Ladies' Home Journal

Number of Years the Firms Continued to Advertise.	Average Number of Lines Used Annually by Each Firm.
1 year	56 lines
2 years	116 lines
3 years	168 lines
4 years	194 lines
5 years	192 lines
6 years	262 lines
7 years	218 lines
8 years	600 lines

This would seem to indicate that in general if a firm uses 56 lines annually in the Ladies' Home Journal the results will be so unsatisfactory that it will not try it again. If it uses 116 lines annually it will be encouraged to attempt it the second year, but will then drop out. If, on the other hand, it uses 600 lines annually the results will be so satisfactory that it will continue to use the same magazine indefinitely. (A very large number of the firms who continued in eight years continued in for a longer time.)

There were but 1,247 firms included in the data presented above. Other data were secured from the entire number of firms advertising in the Ladies' Home Journal, the Delineator, Harper's, and Scribner's for certain periods, but inasmuch as the data from all these merely confirm those presented above they are not added here.

Successful Advertising Not Discontinued

Advertisers are in general wise business men and are usually able to tell whether their advertising pays or not. If it pays, they continue it; if it does not pay, they cease to advertise. Every one can think of an occasional exception, but in general the statement is correct. That class of advertising which is the most successful is the class most likely to be continued. That class which is the least successful is the least likely to be continued. The survival of the fittest is as true in advertising as it is in organic nature. If large spaces are more valuable in proportion to their size than small spaces, we should expect to find the larger spaces surviving. If the smaller spaces are more valuable in proportion to their size we should expect to find the small spaces surviving.

What has been the experience of advertisers — especially of magazine advertisers — on this point? It is a debated question whether there is a growing tendency toward larger or smaller advertisements. In articles in magazines for business men the statement is often made that we are finding it unnecessary to use large spaces, but that small spaces well filled are the more profitable.

Results of Extensive Investigations

To find out definitely what the tendency is in regard to the use of space, several investigations have been carried on. We shall, however, confine the discussion to the question as it manifests itself in the Century Magazine. We have chosen the Century because it is one of the best advertising mediums, because it has had one of the most consistent histories and because all the files have been made available from the first issue of the magazine. We have conducted similar investigations, but in a less thorough manner, with several of the leading advertising mediums in America. In each one of these investigations we have secured results similar to those presented below from the Century. The following data, therefore, show a general tendency; so the data and discussion are not to be interpreted as having any special reference to the Century Magazine. In preparing the tabulation, school announcements and announcements made by the publishers of the magazine were disregarded.

In the following table the first column indicates the year, the second column the total number of pages devoted to commercial advertising during that year in the Century Magazine, the third column the total number of firms advertising in the magazine that year the fourth the average number of lines used by each firm during the year, the fifth the average number of lines in each advertisement appearing in the magazine for that year, the sixth the average number of times each firm advertised in the Century for that year.

Several things in this tabulation are worthy of careful consideration. The total number of pages devoted to advertising has been increasing very rapidly till now there are over one thousand pages devoted to advertising annually as compared with two hundred pages which was the approximate amount during the first ten years of the existence of the magazine. With the exception of the years of financial distress in the nineties almost every year has shown an increase over the preceding year. The growth has been so constant and has been sustained for so many years that it would seem to be nothing more than a normal growth. The increase is seen to be greatest in the years of prosperity, while during the years of depression there is usually a decrease.

Increased Space Devoted to Advertising

The second point to be considered in the tabulation is the number of firms which advertised in the magazine in the years from 1870 to 1907. It will be noticed that during the first ten years there were about two hundred firms advertising. From 1880 to 1890 the increase was extremely rapid. In 1880 there were but 293 firms, while in 1890 there were 910

Number of Advertisers Decreasing

Date.	Total number of pages of commercial advertising for each year in the Century Magazine.	Total number of different firms advertising during each year in the Century Magazine.	Average number of lines used by each advertiser during the twelve months in the Century Magazine.	Average number of lines in each advertisement appearing in the Century Magazine for the year indicated.	Average number of times each firm advertised during the year in the Century Magazine.
1870	33	66	112		
1871	154	186	185		
1872	183	251	163	38	4.22
1873	196	300	146	32	4.46
1874	189	341	124	30	4.68
1875	231	318	162	31	5.65
1876	162	273	132	30	4.41
1877	178	230	173	38	4.49
1878	202	221	205	57	3.56
1879	208	224	208	63	3.30
1880	244	293	186	61	3.04
1881	312	299	233	66	3.50
1882	355	351	226	74	3.53
1883	395	463	191	59	3.23
1884	427	489	195	54	3.60
1885	446	662	150	43	3.51
1886	634	656	214	54	3.91
1887	662	731	202	51	3.96
1888	873	725	269	63	4.24
1889	893	779	256	60	4.21
1890	1061	910	261	50	4.50
1891	1173	900	292	60	4.78
1892	1178	840	314	61	5.08
1893	1141	770	332	64	5.18
1894	919	678	304	64	4.84
1895	902	638	317	61	5.13
1896	831	605	308	65	4.72
1897	828	539	332	68	4.82
1898	782	483	363	68	4.68
1899	954	473	452	77	4.90
1900	946	489	433	88	4.90
1901	921	437	472	98	4.82
1902	988	455	486	112	4.34
1903	1135	479	531	117	4.54
1904	1064	427	558	119	4.69
1905	1198	393	683	114	5.09
1906	1174	402	654	140	4.67
1907	1056	364	650	151	4.30

firms advertising in the same magazine. From 1890 there has been a rapid falling off till in 1907 there were but 364 firms advertising in the magazine. During the year 1907 fewer firms were advertising in this magazine than for any year for a quarter of a century. Although the decrease has been but slight during the recent prosperous years, we can but wonder what will happen when a period of years comes which is less prosperous, such years, for instance, as those of the early nineties when the number of firms was so greatly reduced.

The question naturally arises as to the possibility of nine hundred firms advertising successfully during a single year in the same magazine. Perhaps it is possible, but it certainly has not been attained in 1890–1907; otherwise the firms would not have discontinued their contracts. Certain advertising managers have seen the difficulty of crowding so many advertisements into the two groups at the front and the end of the magazines and have sought to avoid the difficulty by scattering the advertisements through the reading matter. In this way all advertisements are in some magazines placed "next to reading matter." The proof is not conclusive that this method of scattering the advertisements is of any great advantage.

Larger Space Being Used

The point made clear by the fourth column of the table is that of the increase in the amount of space used annually by each advertiser. The fifth and sixth columns show that this increase is not due to the more frequent insertion of advertisements but to the increased size of the individual advertisements. Until 1890 each firm used on the average approximately one page annually. About the year 1890 the real struggle for existence set in among advertisements, and that is the time to which we must look for the survival of the fittest. If the small advertisements had been the most profitable, then the users of small spaces would have survived and would have appeared in the following years. Such, however, is not the case. In that fierce struggle the small spaces proved to be incapable of competing with the larger spaces, and we find in the succeeding years that the users of small spaces grew gradually less. This is shown by the fact that although the number of advertisers has decreased, the amount of space used has increased. This process is still continuing. The year 1907 was almost identical with the year 1890 as to the total advertising space, but showed a decrease of 60 per cent. in the number of firms advertising, while the average amount of space used by each advertiser has increased 150 per cent. This pronounced increase in space and decrease in the number of advertisers is perhaps the most astounding fact observed in the development of advertising in America.

Need for Experts in Advertising

It is not to be assumed that the size of a poor advertisement will keep it from failure any more than the age of a consumptive will be of supreme moment in determining his probable length of life. It is also not to be assumed that all classes of merchandise can use full pages with profit and that no classes of business can be more successful when using small spaces than when using larger ones. The point which should be emphasized is that the size of an advertisement is one of the vital elements and that every advertising agent or manager should be an advertising expert and should be able to give advice as to the size of an advertisement which would be the most profitable to present any particular firm with any particular text and illustration.

The advertising agents and managers should not only be experts, able to give such advice, but they should have such confidence in their own judgments that they would refuse to handle the business of any firm which insisted on using spaces which court failure. Every failure is an injury to the advertising medium, and the results of a failure should be looked upon as such a serious matter that periodicals which proved unprofitable in a large proportion of cases would be avoided. Physicians are regarded as experts along a certain line, and if patients refuse to follow their advice they not infrequently refuse to treat them further. The lawyer is an expert along another line and he assumes his client will take his advice, and is ordinarily correct in his assumption. There is no good reason why the advertising manager or agent should not be looked upon in the same way. If he is sincere in his judgments, and if he has taken account of the advertising experience of the many and not of the few, he should be able to assist the prospective advertiser in avoiding the pitfalls which have been the destruction of a very large proportion of all firms that have attempted to advertise.

Advertising can no longer be said to be in its infancy. It has now reached mature years, and it is high time that the professional advertising men should awake to their responsibility and display the same wisdom that is displayed by the physician and the lawyer. A physician prides himself not only in the number of his patients, but also in the low death rate of his patients. I believe that the day is soon coming, and indeed is now here, when the advertising managers of our periodicals will pride themselves in the low mortality rate of their advertisers rather than in the total number of advertising pages appearing monthly. In the end the magazine which has the lowest mortality rate will of course be the most profitable both to the buyer and to the seller of space. Because of the psychological effect produced by the larger spaces, and because of the comparative values of large and of small spaces as given above, it is evident that one of the duties of the advertising manager and agent is to insist on the use of adequate space and to be able to advise what is adequate space in any particular case.

XIV
THE PSYCHOLOGY OF FOOD ADVERTISING

The "Taste" of Foods

THE *taste* of foods is partially a matter of sentiment and imagination. This is largely true of all foods, but is particularly applicable to foods as served by our modern chefs. Our rural ancestors were engaged long hours of the day in strenuous toil in the open air. For them eating was merely to relieve the pangs of hunger. Pork and beans would cause their mouths to "water," and would be a more tempting morsel to them than are the best-prepared dishes of our gastronomic artists to us. Times have changed. We have turned from a rural population living out of doors into an urban population of sedentary habits. This change is manifesting itself yearly in the alterations which are being wrought in our food consumption. The cruder, grosser and unesthetic foods are finding fewer consumers, while those foods are finding a readier market which are more delicate in texture and more elegant and esthetic in appearance. Of all kinds of meat, pork is the one that is the least pleasing to the eye. It does not lend itself easily to any form of garniture, and it is not surprising that in the fifty years from 1850 to 1900 the American people had become more and more infrequent eaters of pork. In 1850 each inhabitant of the land ate on the average considerably more than one hog. In 1900 each inhabitant ate considerably less than one-half of a hog. This is a falling off of over 60 per cent. Of all the meat foods, eggs are perhaps the most pleasing in appearance. They are often used as garniture for other meats and are themselves easily garnished. It is not strange that in this same period of fifty years the use of eggs should be on the increase. The data are not at hand for the entire period, but in 1880 each inhabitant of the United States consumed, on the average, 110 eggs. In 1900 each inhabitant consumed 204 eggs. This is an increase of over 85 per cent. in twenty years, which must be regarded as a most remarkable change for any people to make.

The appetite of our modern urban civilization is much more a matter of sentiment and imagination than was that of our rural ancestors. We all think that we prefer turkey to pork because the *taste* of the turkey is better than that of the pork. We should question the esthetic judgment of a man who would be so bold as to say that the taste of chicken is as good as that of quail. Even if I have such a cold in my head that I can smell nothing. I should greatly prefer maple sirup to sorghum molasses. It seems absurd that there should be any possibility of hesitation in choosing between these articles. The facts are that in each of these alternatives as to choice we are unable to distinguish the difference between the two by *taste* at all.

The "tasting game" has proved itself to be extremely interesting to both old and young. In this game portions of food are given to blindfolded subjects who are then asked to identify the food by eating it. In arranging for this game, the foods should be carefully prepared. The meats should be chopped fine and no seasoning or characteristic dressing of any sort should be used. If these conditions are observed, and if in no extraneous manner the name of the food is suggested, the blindfolded subjects will make the most astounding mistakes in trying to name the most ordinary articles of diet. The following are some of the mistakes which will actually occur: Strawberry sirup may be called peach sirup or sugar sirup. Beef broth may be called chicken broth. The liquid in which cabbage has been boiled may be said to be the liquid from turnips. Malt extract may be called yeast or ale. Veal broth may be called the broth of mutton, beef or chicken. Raw potatoes chopped fine may be thought to be chopped acorns. White bread may be called whole-wheat bread. Boston brown bread may be called corn-meal cake. Beef, veal, pork, turkey, chicken, quail and other meats will be confused in a most astounding manner.

This "tasting game" would be impossible if we really discriminated between our articles of diet by the sense of taste.

We are at once led to inquire for the reasons why we choose one article of food and reject another if their tastes are so similar that we cannot tell them apart when our eyes are closed or blindfolded. Why do we prefer turkey to pork? Of course there are certain cuts of pork which do not resemble certain parts of turkey, but the question has to do only with those parts of turkey and pork which cannot be easily discriminated with closed eyes. The correct answer to the question is that we prefer turkey to pork because turkey is rarer than pork and because there is a certain atmosphere or halo thrown about turkey which is not possessed by pork. We are inclined to think of pork as "unclean," gross and unesthetic. Turkey has enveloped itself in visions of feasts and banquets. It is associated with Thanksgiving and all the pleasant scenes connected therewith. We have seen pictures in which turkey was so garnished that it looked beautiful. Grossness and sensuousness naturally attach themselves to the unesthetic process of eating and to the unesthetic articles of food, but turkey associates itself with our most pleasing thoughts and does not stand out in all its nudity as dead fowl.

Again it may be asked, Why do we prefer quail to chicken? This can be answered in terms similar to those in which we explained the preference for turkey as compared with pork. Quail is rarer than chicken. Furthermore, the quail is associated in our minds with the pleasures of the chase, the open fields, pure air, the copse of woods, vigorous exercise, days spent in agreeable companionship and exhilarating sport. Our ancestors lived by the chase, and we seem to have inherited a fondness and even love for everything connected therewith. It might also be added that quail is served in a more elegant form than chicken. The garnish is a large part of a quail, but chicken is likely to be served in its nudity. There is a delicacy and yet a plumpness about the quail which is not to be found in a chicken. It will be noticed that all these points of superiority of quail over chicken are independent of taste; yet they all have a part in determining our final judgment as to the *taste* of the meat.

The American people have been long years in creating this sentiment in favor of the turkey and the quail, but it is well established, and it will make turkey and quail to be desired even when other meats equally good in taste are rejected.

The man who has food-stuffs to sell would be fortunate if he could get his commodity in a class with turkey and quail. Such a result would insure him constant sales at a profitable price. Just as we are willing to pay more for turkey and quail than we are for pork and chicken, so we would be willing to pay more for any article of food which could be presented to us in such an appetizing atmosphere as they are.

Creating an "Atmosphere" for a Food Product

The questions which naturally arise in the mind of the advertiser are, Can I create such a sentiment in favor of my commodity that it will be seen enshrined in sentiment? Has a glamour ever been created for an article of merchandise by advertising? This last question must certainly be answered in the affirmative. If the advertisements of Ivory Soap

(No. 1) have accomplished anything, it is this very thing. All of these advertisements have been of one class for a quarter of a century. They all bring out the one point of spotless elegance. These advertisements have created an atmosphere, and when I think

No. 1.— This advertisement assists in creating an atmosphere of spotless elegance about Ivory Soap.

of Ivory Soap a halo of spotless elegance envelops it, and I do not think of it merely as a prosaic chunk of fat and alkali. I have had this idea of spotless elegance so thoroughly associated with Ivory Soap by means of these many advertisements that I actually enjoy using Ivory Soap more than I would if the soap had not been thus advertised. The advertising of this soap not only induces me to buy it, but it influences me in my judgment of the soap after I have bought it.

Another advertising campaign which is to be likened

No. 2.— This advertisement attempts to associate with the Chickering Piano an atmosphere of sumptuous elegance.

to that of Ivory Soap is that of the Chickering Piano (No. 2). These advertisements, like those of Ivory Soap, often seem to say so little and at times it really seems that they squander their space by filling almost the entire page with the illustration and by saying so little directly about their merchandise. They are alike in that the goods advertised are not thrust out into the foreground of the illustration. The Chickering Piano may, indeed, be the central part of the cut, but other articles of furniture, etc., are emphasized in a manner which seems to detract from the piano. Many advertisements of the Chickering Piano are evidently devised to represent the piano as an article of furniture in a home which is most sumptuously and tastefully furnished. We are left to draw the conclusion for ourselves that if persons with such elegant homes choose the Chickering it must be good enough for us. The piano is set most artfully in this atmosphere of cultured refinement and elegance. Most pianos are advertised merely *as pianos,* and I can think of them as such, but I find that my thought of the Chickering is biased by this air of elegance which hovers over it.

It seems to me that the sentiment created in favor of Ivory Soap and Chickering Pianos is quite comparable to that which exists in favor of turkey and quail. So far as I am concerned no advertiser of foodstuffs has quite equaled Ivory Soap and the Chickering Piano in creating a favorable sentiment or atmosphere in favor of his commodity. The firm which has come the nearest to it is the National Biscuit Company. Their advertisements of Nabisco (No. 3) are most excellent in that they create an atmosphere which is exactly suited to the article advertised. Delicacy and purity, even bordering on the romantic and sentimental, are the qualities which we all feel as we look at the advertisements or read them. These advertisements have been so successful with me that when I eat a Nabisco I seem to get a sentimental or romantic taste out of it. If while in the dark, I were given a

No. 3.— This advertisement attempts to associate with Nabisco an atmosphere of romance and sentiment.

new flavor of Nabisco, and if I did not know what it was, it would not taste so good as it would under normal conditions. I enjoy Nabisco wafers more because of these advertisements than I should if I had not seen them. Sentiment is not easily or quickly engendered, but if this style of advertising is continued I anticipate that Nabisco sugar wafers will taste better and better with each succeeding appearance of a good advertisement.

A soda-cracker is one of the most prosaic things imaginable, and nothing kills the flavor of an article

No. 4.—This advertisement attempts to associate with a soda-cracker an atmosphere of patriotism.

of diet more than this feeling of the commonplace and the lack of poetical or esthetic sentiment. The National Biscuit Company is undertaking a big task when it attempts to weave poetical associations about Uneeda Biscuit (No. 1). The attempts thus far have been but half-hearted and infrequent. The reproduced illustration shown herewith (No. 4) is a very good attempt to give the Uneeda Biscuit a connection with man's higher nature. If the firm is able to create a sentimental setting, or to associate the soda-cracker with something patriotic, or with something of that sort, it will add immensely to the "taste" of the commodity.

There are a few advertisers of food products who are trying to create an appetizing halo and to spread it over their goods, but in general, food advertisements are woefully weak at this point. If my appreciation of a soap or a piano can be increased by advertising, then most assuredly there is a great field for profitable endeavor for the advertiser of food-stuffs. Nothing is influenced by sentiment and imagination more than the sense of taste. Whether I like an article of food or not often depends upon what I think of the food before I taste it. Here is the advertiser's opportunity. He is able to influence me to buy the goods, and then his advertisements may make me like the taste of the goods after I have bought them. Whether his goods will be classed with "pork" or with "turkey" depends not only on the real taste of the food-stuff, but also upon the efficacy of the advertisements in creating the favorable atmosphere.

When we are pleased we are open to suggestions and are easily induced to act. When we are displeased, we become insensible to appeals, and are over-cautious in our actions. One of the functions of the advertiser is to please the prospective customers and in every way possible to knit agreeable suggestions about the product offered for sale.

Pleasure Increases Demand for Foods

Most persons choose their foods wholly upon the standard of taste. They choose that which tastes good while they are eating it, and refuse that which is displeasing to the palate. The savory morsel is eaten without thought as to its chemical constituents.

Perhaps in no form of advertising is it so necessary to please the prospective customer as in food advertising. Pleasure stimulates the appetite, and pleasure is the standard of choice. The advertiser of food products should therefore present only the most pleasing suggestions, and he should depict his food product in the most appetizing manner possible.

It is true that certain foods are bought because of their medicinal properties, but such foods should be regarded as medicine rather than as food. The trend of our diet is not dependent upon any one thing. A careful study of the changed food fashions will discover many agencies at work, but among others will certainly be found the appearance of the food stuff. The package, can, bag, basket, bottle, or whatever is used to encase the goods as sold and delivered, must be regarded as an integral part of the food stuff, and as an efficient factor in determining whether the goods will be consumed in increasing or decreasing quantities. How much more appetizing are crackers packed in a box than the same crackers sold in bulk! Who will say how much is due to the form of the box in the enormous increase of crackers in America during the last few years! Would the American public ever have taken kindly to the cereal breakfast food if we had been compelled to buy it in the bulk?

The housewife purchases the provisions for the table. In her mind the package is intimately associated with the contents. She knows that a meal does not taste good unless the linen is spotless and the service more or less formal and ceremonious. The package in which the goods are delivered is as surely associated with the food as is the linen of the table and all the other articles of service. The modern housewife is insisting on a beautiful dining-room, the best of linen and artistically decorated china. The glassware must be cut-glass and the silver of the most improved pattern. The table must be decorated and the individual dishes garnished. The housewife who is insisting on all these details is the one the merchant should have in mind when he is planning for the sale of his goods. She wants those articles of food which come in neat packages and which can be served in neat and elegant form. In her mind the appearance is an essential part of the taste, and she does not believe that a food can be appetizing unless it looks as if it were.

This same modern housewife predetermines her choice of foods by what she knows of them in advance. Her ideas may be molded by advertising, for this process is at work daily in all our homes. Like the housewives, we all form an idea of a food by the advertisements of it which we have seen, even if we have not read them. If the advertisment looks pleasing and if the food is there presented in an appetizing manner, we believe that the food itself will be all right and we are prejudiced in favor of it.

No. 5.— An over crowded advertisement; the promiscuous abundance kills the appetite for food.

One thing that spoils the looks of food products is having them piled up in a confused mass. A table which contains many articles of food at once is not inviting to the epicure. We like to have our meals served in courses, and prefer many light courses rather than a few heavy ones. The same principle holds with advertisements. Many advertisements which would otherwise be strong are weakened by overcrowding of good things.

No. 6.— A simplification of the wheatlet border. It familiarizes the public with the appearance of the package.

The reduced advertisement of Wheatlet (No. 5) as reproduced herewith is not appetizing, for the appearance of the whole thing is ruined by the multitude of fruits which are thrown promiscuously into the illustration. I think I might like Wheatlet if it were served with any *one* of these fruits, but if it should be presented in such a confusion as this it would not be eaten at all.

The reproduced advertisement of Egg-o-See (No. 6) has adopted the Wheatlet border, but in such a simplified form that it is successful in suggesting wheat and does not overcrowd the illustration.

The method which the house-keepers of the land employ in purchasing foods must be a factor in determining the appropriate form of advertising. In some instances householders make written lists of the goods desired; the order is placed without looking at the goods at all. In other instances the order is sent by telephone or by a messenger. In perhaps the most cases the purchaser enters the grocery store in person. She has her list of purchases but imperfectly made out. As she enters the store she is confronted by rows and tiers of bottles, cans and boxes. Out of this bewildering multitude of packages she is pleased to see certain ones which are known to her. These familiar packages catch her attention more than the scores of unknown ones. The known ones are the packages which she is most likely to purchase, as they catch her attention just at the time she is trying to recall the things of which she may be in need.

Of the two advertisements (Wheatlet and Egg-o-See), the last mentioned emphasizes the appearance of the package, while the advertisement of Wheatlet omits the presentation of the package. At the moment of making the purchases for the week these two commodities might be on the shelf before the purchaser. The reproduced advertisement of Egg-o-See is such that it has made her familiar with the package as it appears on the shelves and it would thus be called to her attention at the critical moment. The advertisement of Wheatlet is not such as would have assisted in familiarizing her with the appearance of the package, and thus it does not assist in attracting her eye to the goods advertised at the moment of decision. While in the grocery store the purchaser does not taste the various articles, but tier upon tier of different goods are presented to her sense of sight. It is by sight that she recognizes the various packages, and an advertising campaign that familiarizes the housekeepers of the nation with the distinguishing appearance of any particular package has done much to increase its sale.

While the public is being made familiar with the food or the food container, a pleasing appeal should also be made to the esthetic nature of the possible customers.

The human race is carnivorous, but it does not like to be reminded of the fact. It is disgusting to think of eating the flesh of dead cows, hogs and sheep. We refuse to use the terms cow-flesh, hog-flesh and sheep-flesh. Our abhorrence of such ideas is registered in our language, and so we use the terms beef, pork and mutton. It is not pleasing to think of eating the flesh of the smaller animals and of fowls, still it is not so

Are We Carnivorous?

abhorrent as the thought of eating the flesh of the larger and domestic animals. Accordingly we still use the same word to denote the live animal and the flesh in such instances as rabbit, squirrel, chicken, goose, etc.

It is quite conceivable that the sight of a dead carcass would whet the appetite of a hyena. The sight of a fat pig might cause the mouth of a wolf to "water." The sight of an animal, whether dead or alive, is not very appetizing to the civilized man or woman. We know that beef is nothing but the flesh of dead cattle, but we refuse to entertain the idea at meal time. Indeed, we have become so cultured that we like to have our meats garnished till they cease to have the appearance of flesh at all. There are whole nations which refuse to eat meat, and vegetarianism in our own country is but an indication of the revolt of the human mind against our carnivorous habits.

As a nation our wealth is increasing rapidly and consequently we are better able to purchase meats now than fifty years ago, yet the government statistics show a great decrease *per capita* in the consumption of meats. We have changed from a rural to an urban population and hence require less meat foods, and what we do eat must always be presented in a pleasing manner and in a way which jars as little as possible against our refined and cultivated natures.

In advertising meats, the fact should never be emphasized that the meat is the flesh of an animal. That point should be taken for granted and passed over as lightly as possible. Certain advertisers have not taken this matter into consideration and press to the front the fact that their meats are the flesh of animals. Thus the reproduced advertisement of Liebig (No. 7) is given up to the emphasizing of the point that this extract is secured from the carcasses of beautiful steers. This advertisement makes no one hungry for Liebig Company's extract of beef. The advertisement is intended to make the public

Meat Advertisements vs. Our Sensibilities

No. 7.— This advertisement makes no one hungry for extract of beef.

familiar with the Liebig trade-mark, and the criticism is therefore directed against the choice of such a trademark rather than against this special advertisement, which is but a presentation of the trade-mark. The reproduced advertisement of Armour & Co. (No. 8) does not present an animal in its entirety, but it represents too much of it. The carcasses as shown in the advertisement are too large to tempt our appetites and the general effect is rather disgusting. If smaller

No. 8.—This advertisement associates Armour's meat with the carcasses of dead animals.

pieces of meat had been shown, the result would have been entirely different.

The reproduced advertisement of Armour's potted

ham and ox tongue (No. 9) is perhaps one of the most pleasing advertisements of meats that has appeared in our magazines. No one can look at the ad-

No. 9.— This advertisement increases the appetite for Armour's meat.

vertisement without being impressed with the desirability of these products. The meat is presented in small pieces and is garnished till it is hardly recognizable. Such an advertisement creates a demand for the goods and prejudices the customers in their favor, and the ham and ox tongue will taste better to the customer after he has seen this advertisement. This

No. 10.— A slimy frog associated with White Star coffee kills the desire for coffee.

would be a better advertisement for Armour & Co. if the can were shown in which this meat had been purchased. The border might include a cut of the container and the total effect be rendered none the less artistic.

Associating Foods With Animals

We not only object to thinking of ourselves as carnivorous but we object to having animals connected in any way with our foods. The reproduced advertisement of White Star Coffee (No. 10) is in every way disgusting. Frogs are inherently uncanny to most persons, and to see them here as the

No. 11.—He seems to like it and I imagine that it is excellent.

representatives of a particular brand of coffee serves but to instil a dislike and even abhorrence for the product. This advertisement never made anyone eager for a cup of coffee. It does not create a demand for coffee and in the cases where the demand already exists it does not convince the casual observer that White Star Coffee is particularly desirable. It is one

No. 12.— An example of waste in advertising.

of the most silly and destructive advertisements appearing in our current magazines. The other reproduced advertisement of the same brand of coffee (No. 11) is in no way objectionable and is a great improvement in point of display over the first one.

Ordinarily we feed the animals what we do not care to eat ourselves, and the assumption is that that which is good enough for the beasts is not fit for men and women. In the reproduced advertisement of Korn Krisp (No. 12) the food is represented as being fed to the fowls. The assumption would be that it is a food especially adapted to their taste, and I should not want to eat it myself. Even the young goose seems to be disgorging the food for some unexplained reason! Here we have evidence of an amateur advertiser who was enamoured with his play on the words, "it fills the bill," and who was willing to pay for the exploitation of his joke under the pretense of an advertisement.

It may be possible that under very exceptional circumstances it would be advisable to introduce an animal in an advertisement of a food product, but it should be done only with great caution and with full realization of the dangers incurred because of the inevitable association between the animal and the food advertised.

Purity and Elegance

The advertiser must seek to associate his food only with purity and elegance. In a sense the advertisement is the representative of the food, and if the advertisement is associated with disgusting or displeasing objects the food is the loser thereby. The advertising pages of many of our cheaper periodicals are nothing better than chambers of horrors. The afflictions of mankind are here depicted in an exaggerated form. The paper is poor, the ink is the cheapest and the make-up is without taste. They are altogether a gruesome sight. Food advertisements in such papers are practically worthless. Even in these papers a few food advertise-

"LOOK PLEASANT, PLEASE."
MALT MARROW
McAVOY MALT EXTRACT DEPT., CHICAGO.

CURED, SATISFIED PATIENTS
Are Convincing Proof of Dr. Reynolds' Unfailing Methods to Effect Life-long Cures for BLOOD POISON, SKIN DISEASES, VARICOCELE, HYDROCELE, NERVOUS DECLINE, "WEAKNESS," PILES, FISTULA, RUPTURE, KIDNEY and BLADDER AFFECTIONS.
No Money Required to Commence Treatment
REMEMBER
COST YOU NOTHING
CURE OR NO CHARGE
CONSULTATION FREE AND INVITED

BLOOD POISON
COOK REMEDY CO.

Every Woman
is interested and should know about the wonderful Marvel Whirling Spray Douche
MARVEL CO., Room 20b, Times Building, N. Y.

Asthma
CURED TO STAY CURED.
P. HAROLD HAYES, Buffalo, N. Y.

Pimples, Blackheads, Large pores, eruptions and all disorders affecting the skin and scalp permanently cured.
JOHN H. WOODBURY D. I.

CREME MARQUISE
MRS. M. E. FRANCIS.

ARMOUR'S "STAR" THE HAM WHAT AM

Hood's Sarsaparilla
Strengthens the kidneys, stimulates the liver, cures Backache, biliousness, etc.

YE OLDE INN ALE
KEELEY BREWING CO., Chicago, Ill.

Old Underoof Rye

DUFFY'S PURE MALT WHISKEY
CURES CONSUMPTION.

Lighten the Ills of Humanity.

No. 13.— Food advertisements ruined by the make-up of the paper.

ments are found, but, fortunately, there are only a few. In these cheaper forms of publications the majority of advertisements are likely to be of patent medicines or of forms of investments. The medicines are advertised by depicting the unwholesome aspects of life, and the investments are usually of a questionable sort. These advertisements of patent medicines and investment schemes make the readers suspicious and hence they are in a condition of mind which leads them to suspect the foods advertised as being adulterated and impure.

Even good daily papers are open to this criticism. No. 13 is a reproduction of a section of one of the best American dailies. The food advertisements are here associated with " skin diseases," " asthma," " consumption," " blood poison," " whirling spray douche," " pimples," " eruptions," " backaches," and other ills and unappetizing suggestions. What value is the advertisement of Malt Marrow and of Armour's Star Ham in such an environment? Until the daily papers have more to offer than such position as is indicated by No. 13 they certainly are not preferred media for food advertisers.

XV

THE UNCONSCIOUS INFLUENCE IN STREET RAILWAY ADVERTISING

EVERY form of advertising has its particular psychological effect, and the medium which the merchant should choose depends upon many conditions. Foremost among such conditions are expense, the class of persons to be reached, the quality of goods to be presented, the width of distribution of goods, etc., etc. Equal with these conditions, however, the advertiser should consider the peculiar psychological effect of each particular form. The monthly magazine, the weeklies and the dailies carry authority which is lacking in other forms. These publications are held in high repute in the household, and advertisements appearing in them are benefited by this confidence which is bestowed upon everything appearing in them. Posters, bill-boards, painted signs and similar forms of advertising admit of extensive display within a prescribed area and have great attention value. Booklets, circulars and similar forms of advertising admit of complete descriptions and may be put in the hands of only those who are interested in the commodity offered for sale. They appeal to the reason in a way not surpassed by any form of printed advertising.

The psychological effect of street car advertising is not generally recognized and in this presentation there is no attempt to praise one form of advertising and to decry all others, but inasmuch as the psychological effects of other forms are recognized and that of street car advertising is frequently not recognized, this latter is selected for fuller presentation.

Importance of Time

Our minds are constantly subjected to influences of which we have no knowledge. We are led to form opinions and judgments by influences which we should reject if we were aware of them. After we have decided upon a certain line of action, we frequently attempt to justify ourselves in our own eyes, and so we discover certain logical reasons for our actions and assume them to have been the true cause, when in reality they had nothing to do with it. The importance of these undiscovered causes in our every-day thinking and acting may be illustrated by the following example.

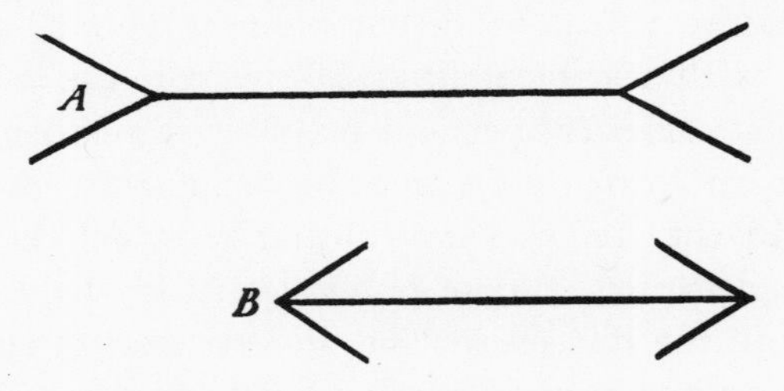

Lines A and B are of equal length, although A seems longer. Now why do we reach the conclusion that A is longer than B, when in reality such is not the case? If they are the same length, and we see them in a clear light, we should expect that they would appear to be as they actually are. The accepted explanation of this illusion is that there are, entering into the judgment, certain imperceptible causes which make us see the lines as of different length. This explanation was not discovered till recent years, but it has been proved to be correct. In judging the length of lines we run our eyes over them, and so get a sensation from the contraction of the muscles of the eyes. We judge of the length of lines by the amount of this sensation derived from contracting the muscles which move the eyes. If two lines are the same distance from us and are the same length, our eyes will ordinarily move equal distances in traversing their lengths. If two lines are equally distant from us, and one longer than the other, we ordinarily have to move our eyes farther in estimating the length of the longer one than in estimating the length of the shorter one. We are not aware of the sensations received from these movements of our eyes, and yet we estimate lengths of lines by them. The peculiar construction of the lines A and B induces the eye to move farther in estimating the length of A. We therefore assume that A is longer than B because our eyes move farther in estimating its length than in estimating the length of B.

The street railway advertiser controls an unrecognized force which is similar to that just described in the estimation of the length of lines. The arrow pointing toward the line as shown in A causes us all to overestimate the magnitude of the line; and there is a factor present in street railway advertising which causes us to be influenced by it more than would seem possible. There has been much poor street railway advertising, and yet the results have been phenomenally great. Some recent tests of the extent to which passengers had been influenced by such advertising showed most conclusively that there was an unrecognized power in it. A study of the situation discloses the fact that this unconscious influence is none other than *TIME* which manifests itself in three phases as presented below.

Time Whiled Away

As a result of investigations upon magazine and newspaper advertising the conclusion was reached that on the average only ten per cent. of the time devoted to newspapers and magazines was spent in looking at the advertisements. (For a fuller account of the investigation see Chapter X.) As a conclusion deduced from these results it was recommended that advertisements should be so constructed that the gist of each could be comprehended at a glance, for most advertisements in newspapers and magazines receive no more than a glance from the average reader. The ordinary reader of newspapers and magazines *glances* at all of the advertising pages and sees all the *larger and more striking* advertisements. There are many exceptions to this. There are persons who read all the advertisements and there are others who glance at but few of them. Magazines and newspapers have become so numerous and the daily duties so pressing that we cannot take time to read all the advertisements, and so we devote but few minutes to them, and in those few minutes we see a great number. We cannot afford the time to do more.

The case is different with street railway advertising. Here there is no shortage of time. There is sufficient opportunity to see every person in the car and to devote as much time to the process as good breeding will allow. Thereafter one is compelled to look at the floor or else above the heads of the passengers. One cannot read a newspaper on a crowded car — I am acquainted only with crowded cars. Neither is it practicable to read a book or magazine on a jolting car — I am acquainted only with such. To attempt to look out of a window opposite to you causes the lady opposite to wonder at your rudeness in staring at her, for to look out of the window the eyes are directed so nearly at the face of some passenger that one's intentions are misjudged. In defense of one's good breeding and to drive away the weariness of the ride many a passenger is compelled to turn his gaze on the placards which adorn the sides of the car. The passenger has for once an abundance of time. He reads the card and then reads it again because he has nothing else to do. This may be very silly, but what of it? It offers a diversion, and anything is better than looking at the floor, counting the number of passengers, or watching the conductor ring up the fares.

The amount of time spent in riding on street cars in America is far beyond the conception of most persons. Statistics show that in the United States in the single year of 1902 about 5,000 million cash fares were collected for passengers on street cars. In addition to these cash fares there were many transfers and passes. The figures for the year 1907 are very much in excess of those for 1902. In the average American city the number of fares collected on street cars equals about 66 per cent. of the total population of the city. There are no data available for the length of time consumed by an average street car ride. Fifteen minutes may be regarded as a fair estimate. Upon this estimate each inhabitant of our cities spends on the average as much as ten minutes a day in a street car. These rides become very monotonous; the passengers' minds are not occupied, and very much more time is whiled away by looking at the advertisements than we are aware of.

Time Secures Forgetfulness of Source of Information

One young lady asserted that she had never looked at any of the cards in the cars in which she had been riding for years. When questioned further, it appeared that she knew by heart almost every advertisement appearing on the line (Chicago and Evanston line), and that the goods advertised had won her highest esteem. She was not aware of the fact that she had been studying the advertisements, and flatly resented the suggestion that she had been influenced by them. Some of the goods advertised were known to her only by these advertisements, yet she supposed that they had nothing to do with her esteem of the goods. She supposed that she had always known them, that they were used in her home, or that they had been recommended to her. She did not remember when she had first heard of them.

It has been said that we have learned nothing perfectly until we have forgotten how we learned it. This has a special application to advertising. An advertisement has not accomplished its mission till it has instructed the possible customer concerning the goods and then has caused him to forget where he received his instruction. This is especially important in street car advertising. The information which we receive from the card in the street car soon becomes a part of us, and we forget where we received it.

This forgetfulness of the source of our information is due to the interval which has elapsed between the first time the advertisement was seen and the present. The more frequently the advertisement is seen, the more rapidly will the memory of the first appearance fade and leave us with the feeling that we have always known the goods advertised, and that the advertisement itself is no essential part of our information. [This point is more fully developed in Chapter VI, Suggestion.]

Time Increases Our Appreciation

The element of *time* as it enters the problem of advertising is recognized to a limited extent in the two phases thus far discussed, but there is another phase and one of even more importance which has, to the writer's knowledge, never been mentioned in connection with advertising. We devote the most time to those subjects which we regard as the most important. My profession takes most of my thought, the lacing of my shoes very little. Ideas which impress me as important cause me to think of them for lengthy periods of time. Ideas which seem insignificant are dismissed immediately from my mind.

This element is recognized by every skilful public speaker. He speaks rapidly that which he wishes us to consider as of little importance. He speaks slowly that which he wishes us to regard as of special significance. We weigh the importance of his statements and estimate their value in terms of the time which he gives to each.

In poetry, thoughts which are trivial or of minor importance are expressed by rapid movements. Ideas which are of more importance and which are supposed to call forth much thought from the reader are expressed in slow movements. This same principle holds in music. Music which means much — which suggests many thoughts, which is sublime, deep or large — all such music is written in slow time. The so-called "rag-time" is assumed to have no meaning; it is not supposed to suggest lines of thought. It has no intrinsic importance and is consequently appropriately expressed in fast time.

In the case of the orator, the poet and the musician the effect is produced by this unrecognized element of time. That which holds our thought for a longer time seems to us to be important; that which we hurry over seems unimportant. The orator, the poet and the musician have simply accommodated themselves to our intuitive method of thinking and have been successful because they have conformed their expressions to the human method of thought.

As was shown above, the passengers on street railways have but little to distract their attention. They go over the same road so frequently that the streets passed through cease to be interesting. Since newspapers and magazines cannot be easily read, the cards have but few rivals for attention. Even those who have but little interest in the advertisements find that they glance at the cards frequently and that the eyes rest on a single card for a considerable length of time. The same card may be read or glanced at daily for as long a time as the card is left in the car. The sum total of the time thus devoted to the card is as great as the amount of time that we devote to many of our important interests. Under ordinary circumstances we bestow thought upon objects in proportion to their importance. This is not an absolute rule, of course, but it expresses a principle. The reverse of this principle is not recognized by us at all and yet it is of primal importance.

That which occupies our minds for a great amount of time assumes thereby an importance which may be out of all proportion to its real value. Illustrations of this fact are to be found on every hand. The mother is likely to think the most of the child which has caused her the most thought. The sickly child occupies her mind more than the well one, and this accounts for the fact that she attributes to the sickly child an importance far beyond its real worth. Our old schoolbooks, upon which we were compelled to bestow so many hours of study, in later years assume a value in our eyes far in excess of their real merit. The goods which through their advertisements have occupied our minds for long periods of time assume in our minds an importance which is often far in excess of anything which would have been anticipated by one who was not familiar with the peculiar power here described. In estimating the relative values of two competing lines of goods, I assume that my judgment is based on the goods themselves as they are presented to my reason. I am not aware of the fact that I am prejudiced in favor of the goods that have occupied my mind the longest periods of time. Yet it is as certain that this element of time has biased my judgment of the relative values of the goods as it is that the eye movement influences my judgment of the lengths of lines.

Advertisements in newspapers and magazines are seen by a great number of the readers, but the time devoted to any particular advertisement is very small, unless there is a special interest in the advertisement.

There is indeed no form of advertising which is presented to such a large number of possible purchasers for such a long period of time and so frequently as is the advertising in street railway cars. In most other forms of advertising we devote to any particular advertisement only as much time as we think it is worth. In street railway advertising we devote longer time than we really think is due to the advertisements, and then we turn around and estimate the value of the goods advertised by the amount of time that we have devoted to the advertisement. This is the psychological explanation of the amazing potency of this particular form of advertising.

XVI

THE QUESTIONNAIRE METHOD IN ADVERTISING

ILLUSTRATED BY AN INVESTIGATION UPON NEWSPAPERS

EXPERIENCE is the best teacher. Methods that enable one to make the greatest use of one's own experience are valuable. Methods that make the experiences of others also available are even more valuable.

One of the functions of every science is to develop methods that are useful for investigating problems which concern that particular science. One of the methods that modern psychology has developed is the so-called Questionnaire Method. This method has many defects, but it has the inestimable value of assisting the investigator to take advantage of the experiences of a great number of individuals.

The questionnaire method is used to secure the concensus and the diversity of many individual opinions. A single question or a set of questions is presented to any desired group of persons. The answers to the questions are derived from the experiences of those who are to answer them. If the questions call for the description of simple unemotional events, reliance may be put in the answers received from all sincere respondents. If the answers call for a difficult analysis of motives and interests, less reliance can be placed in any single answer and greater caution must be used in drawing conclusions based upon the replies.

There are many problems that the advertiser needs to investigate for which the questionnaire method alone is available. A single illustration will indicate how such questions arise, how they may be investigated, and will also present a mass of information concerning newspapers that is of interest and profit to advertisers.

The Problems for Research.

A prominent advertising man was planning copy to be used on street-car cards designed to secure new subscribers to newspapers. The campaign was to be conducted in different American cities in the interest of local papers, but in each case the attempt was to be made to reach the best citizens of the city. The two following questions naturally suggested themselves: *What is there in the modern newspaper that appeals to the better classes of society, and what motives should be appealed to in inducing them to begin a subscription?* The problems here raised are clearly psychological and subject to the questionnaire method, which was employed in investigating them.

A carefully selected list was prepared containing the names of 4,000 of the most prominent business and professional men of Chicago. An attempt was made to include what could fairly be said to be the best citizens of Chicago. The number was so large that it contained a fully representative group. For the purpose of comparison, another list of 1,000 names was prepared. This list contained the names of men from very different classes of society, but all, with few exceptions, were adult men. The questionnaire as reproduced herewith was mailed to the 5,000 names constituting the two lists.

I. What Chicago daily or dailies do you read?................

II. Which one do you prefer?................................

III. State in order the five features of your paper which interest you most. (For example, politics, society, finance, sporting, foreign news, local news, special articles, romance and storiettes, cartoons, advertisements, art, music and book reviews, moral or ethical tone, editorials, brevity, accuracy, etc.)

1............................
2............................
3............................
4............................
5............................

IV. Do you spend on an average as much as 15 minutes daily reading a Chicago paper?............................

V. What induced you to begin the subscription of the paper or papers which you are now taking?....................
....

VI. Were you ever induced by means of a premium or prize to subscribe for a Chicago paper?............... If so, did you resubscribe for the same paper without a premium?...............

....

Answers to these questions are desired from the selected persons to whom they are mailed. The answers are needed in solving a psychological question of interest and may be placed in the stamped envelope enclosed herewith and mailed at once. They will be gratefully received by the sender.

Yours respectfully,

WALTER D. SCOTT,

Director of the Psychological Laboratory,

Northwestern University, Evanston, Illinois.

Replies were received from about 2,300 of the representative business and professional men. The replies from the 1,000 are disregarded in the present chapter; and inasmuch as but approximately 2,000 answered each of the questions, the 2,300 are hereafter referred to as "the 2,000." Those receiving the questionnaire seemed much interested in the research, and although they are very busy men, the answers indicate careful deliberation and the utmost sincerity. Although no place was provided for signatures, a good proportion signed their names to the paper or enclosed a personal, signed letter. A large number of the slips were carefully keyed and even when no signature was attached the author of the replies was known. In all the slips the key indicated at least to which one of the numerous groups the respondent belonged. In case of doubt as to whether the replies were filled out personally by the man to whom the questionnaire was sent, they were rejected as not authentic. No proxies were desired.

Replies Abundant and Valuable.

Over fifty per cent. of those receiving the questionnaire took pains to fill out the blank. This proportion is unusually large and is to be attributed to several causes. A stamped return envelope was enclosed. The subject under investigation was personally interesting. The answers were sought for as a means of "solving a psychological question," and psychology is very popular just at present. The investigator, owing to his university connection, was assumed to be honest and desirous of securing only the facts. The advertiser might have great difficulty in selecting a group of persons whose answers would be significant and yet who would be willing to fill out the blanks. Doubtless in many cases the list would have to be confined to business associates or to personal friends. Haphazard, voluntary answers received in competition for a prize or for the gaining of a paltry reward are not to be compared in value to voluntary replies from a carefully selected list. The difficulty of securing trustworthy replies is so great that the advertiser will usually be compelled to have the investigation carried on by a disinterested person, as it was done in the present instance.

Ordinarily no suggestions should be made as to what answer is expected. If any suggestions are made, that fact should never be forgotten in estimating the results. In the questionnaire reproduced herewith, the amount of space left for answering the first question suggested that the names of but one or two papers were to be written. This doubtless affected the results. Also in connection with the third question a series of answers were suggested. The number of suggestions was made so large that no particular one would have much more effect than the others, and as all probable answers were suggested the results were certainly not greatly changed thereby.

The fact that each individual reads or scans a number of papers daily was brought out clearly by the answers to the first question. (I. What Chicago daily or dailies do you read?) Eighty-six per cent. reported themselves as reading more than a single paper. The space in the questionnaire left for writing the names of the papers read was but a little over one inch in length. In spite of this fact the respondents took pains to write in a number of papers. As stated above, it is quite probable that the inadequate space and, in some cases, the haste of writing the names caused an understatement of the actual number of papers read. As reported, the figures are as follows:

Nunber of Papers Read Daily.

14% read but one paper
46% read two papers
21% read three papers
10% read four papers
3% read five papers
2% read six papers
3% read all the papers (8).

Some of the papers taken by any person are to be regarded as subsidiary and as commanding but little attention. These subsidiary papers contain a large part of the advertisements that are also contained in the preferred papers, which command the most attention. The same advertisement seen in two or three papers may be more effective than if seen in but one; but most advertisers are convinced that it is not worth three times as much to have an advertisement seen in three papers as it is to have it seen in one. The duplication of circulation represents a loss. If the advertiser could pick out the papers that command the most confidence of a relatively large number of readers, he could afford to neglect the subsidiary papers entirely.

The fourth question was, IV. Do you spend on an average as much as fifteen minutes daily reading a Chicago daily?

Time Spent in Reading Daily Papers.

A decided majority seemed to consider fifteen minutes a fair estimate of the time spent in reading the daily papers. Four per cent. answered that they spent less than fifteen minutes daily. Twenty-five per cent. reported a greater amount of time. A few reported as much as two hours, but "just about fifteen minutes" was by far the most common answer. The writers were frequently careful to state that this fifteen minutes was the total time spent in reading all the papers and not the amount spent in reading each of the several papers read. Considering together the total number of papers read and the total amount of time spent in reading them, we reach the conclusion that a very decided majority of these representative business and professional men spend but approximately from five to ten minutes reading any particular paper. These few minutes admit of but the most cursory reading. A favorite program, as reported, is the reading of the head lines, the table of contents, the weather reports, etc. Then if time admits or if anything especially interesting is discovered, attention may be turned for a few seconds or minutes to a more leisurely reading of the articles discovered in the preliminary search.

The papers are glanced through so hurriedly that an advertisement, in order to be seen at all, unless sought for, must be striking in appearance and must announce something in which the reader is particularly interested. Advertisements may be divided into two groups: classified and display advertisements. The classified are read only by those who search for them. The display advertisements are glanced at by a very large number of persons who pick up the paper. The advertisement must tell its story quickly if at all. If the message which it is capable of imparting to those who glance at it is inviting, the advertisement may be selected and read from beginning to end. The advertiser should attempt, however, to construct his advertisement so that a single glance at it may be effective in imparting information and in making an impression even though the advertisement is not to be under observation for more than a few seconds.

Preferences for Individual Papers.

A majority of the respondents answered the second question, naming the preferred paper. (II. Which one do you prefer?) A very respectable minority, however, confessed that they had no preference. Many answered that one paper was preferred for general news, another for cartoons, another for special articles, another for moral tone, etc. Others refused to go on record as preferring any paper and so expressed themselves by saying that one paper was "less objectionable," "less yellow," "less venal," etc., than the others. Particular groups of men displayed considerable uniformity in their preference for a single paper; e.g., the one hundred professional men connected with one educational institution preferred one paper; the business men who were members of an athletic club showed a decided preference for another paper; the business and professional men who were members of one of the most prominent clubs preferred with equal uniformity still a different paper.

The circulation of the evening papers in Chicago is greater than that of the morning papers, and it is probable that they are preferred in more cases than are the morning papers. For business and professional men the reverse is true; among them the morning papers are read in larger numbers and are preferred in more instances than the evening papers. With these men the evening papers are often to be regarded merely as subsidiary. The laboring classes have no time to read a morning paper, but after the day's work is over the evening paper is read and doubtless much more than fifteen minutes is devoted to it. Many business and professional men prefer evening papers and many laboring men prefer the morning papers, but such instances are exceptions rather than the rule.

A majority of business and professional men fail to see advertisements appearing in evening papers and are not greatly affected by those that they do see.

Likewise, probably a majority of the laboring class is unaffected by advertisements appearing in the morning papers. If these statements did not have so many exceptions the advertiser's task would be comparatively simple when it comes to choosing a medium for any particular advertisement. If he wanted to reach the better classes, he would use the morning papers; if he wanted to reach the laboring class, he would employ the evening papers.

The replies from the 2,000 showed somewhat of a uniformity in their selection of a preferred paper, but the most surprising thing was the lack of uniformity. This particular group could not be reached by using anything less than all the papers. Perhaps one-half of them could be reached by a single paper, three-fourths by two papers and over nine-tenths of all by using half the papers.

The chief interest in the investigation centers in the answers to the third question. (III. State in order the five features of your paper that interest you most.)

The Most Interesting Features of a Daily Paper.

To reduce the answers to some sort of a comprehensible unit, the following plan was adopted. A feature that was mentioned as first choice was credited with five points; one mentioned as second choice, four points; one mentioned as third choice, three points; one mentioned as fourth choice, two points; one mentioned as fifth choice, one point. The sum of all these points was arbitrarily assumed to represent the sum total of interest. It was then found what per cent. of this total interest had been credited to politics, editorials and all other features mentioned by any of the respondents. As thus found, the total result for all papers and all respondents is as follows:

	PER CENT.
Local news	17.8
Political news	15.8
Financial news	11.3
Foreign news	9.5
Editorials	9.
General news	7.2
Ethical tone (broadly considered)	6.7
Sporting news	5.8
Cartoons	4.3
Special article	4.3
Music	1.88
Book reviews	1.84
Arrangement	1.4
Society notes	1.4
Drama	1.1
Art	.9
Advertisements	.44
Storiettes	.13
Weather	.1
Humor	.05

Inasmuch as these figures represent the distribution as found for all the papers combined, it would, of course, be anticipated that the same order would not hold exactly for any individual paper. In most particulars there is a pronounced similarity in the distribution of interest in the different papers. This is true, for instance, in the case of local news. In one paper it monopolizes 19.5% of the interest and in the others 18.8%, 18.3%, 17.6%, 14.9%, 13.8%, 12.8%, and 12.1% respectively. In some features the diversity between papers is very great. Thus in one paper 19 per cent. of the interest is in sporting news, in another but 2 per cent. In one paper 19.7 per cent. of the interest is in financial news, in another but 6.9 per cent. These last illustrations from sporting news and finance are exceptional instances, and even in these the extremes are found in the papers that were least often mentioned as the preferred papers. For all the papers and for all the different groups into which the business and professional men were divided the striking fact was the uniformity of interests. Features that were interesting to any group in any paper were usually found to be interesting in all the papers and to all the groups. The features that were most uniformly interesting were the news items, which possessed over 75 per cent. of the total interest. All other features were low in interest with most of the groups and in most of the papers. As is indicated in the tabulation above, advertisements did not seem to attract much attention.

These results make it clear that the Chicago dailies are valued as NEWS papers and as little else. Local news, general news, foreign news, financial news, political news and sporting news — these monopolize the interest of business and professional men. Editorials, storiettes, book reviews, art, music, drama, society — all these combined do not possess so much interest as local news alone. Everyone seemed interested in news, and when cartoons and editorials were mentioned the writers were frequently careful to add that they were interested in these because they were a summary or index of some important news.

Advertisements aiming to secure new subscribers to a newspaper should give most importance to the description of the news service of that particular paper. Other features might be mentioned, but the uniformity with which all groups expressed their interest in the news in each of the papers makes it quite certain that here we have the vital feature of the newspaper and that which gives it its name.

The third question should be considered in connection with the fifth. (V. What induced you to begin the subscription of the paper or papers which you are now taking?) Immediately following the statement of the third question, as printed in the questionaire, suggestive answers were presented. This list of examples acted as a constant suggestion and made it more likely that the answers cited would be given than any original ones. No such suggestions were added to the statement of the fifth question and hence answers to this latter question are more reliable.

Motives for Beginning a Subscription.

While it resulted in the presentation of many different answers, still the uniformity with which the news items were mentioned — observed in the answers to the third question — is even greater here.

Of all the motives that could be classified the following show what per cent. of the total number of times each motive was mentioned:

To keep informed concerning current events..	65%
Ethical tone (including accuracy, etc.)........	10%
Premiums	4%
Cartoons	4%
Special articles	3%
Reputation of paper	1%
Service (best delivery)	1%

All other motives (about twenty in number) received scattering mention.

It is a significant fact that sixty-five per cent. of the business and professional men united in stating that the motive in first subscribing to their chosen papers was the desire to keep informed concerning current events. The following expressions were frequently used and are most suggestive: "to keep in touch with current events," "desire to be informed," "to be informed as to what is going on," "to be up to the times and not a back number," "to be *en rapport* with the world."

In comparison with this desire for news of current events all other motives seem insignificant. News service is the desideratum. If a choice is to be made between papers equally good in news service, then premiums and cartoons or even editorials and storiettes may become the deciding factor.

In waging a campaign to increase the circulation of newspapers the fact should be constantly before the advertiser's mind that people are interested primarily in the news. A description of the methods used by any great paper to secure the news would be a most powerful argument for securing new subscribers. A presentation of all the means employed to avoid mistakes, and hence to present the news accurately, would furnish a theme for further advertisements. A truly educational campaign carried on in the interests of the two themes — completeness of news service and care to present the truth — would increase the circulation of any of the better metropolitan dailies.

Criticism of Daily Papers.

The questionnaire invited no criticisms of daily papers and yet many of these business and professional men volunteered criticisms which they inserted on the sheets of questions or else wrote them in personal letters that were enclosed. There are but few criticisms of the less important features of the papers. There are almost no criticisms of the storiettes, the society notes, the book reviews, the funny columns, etc. All these seem to be as good as desired; nor does the reader express himself as aggrieved by the poor quality or even by the absence of any of them.

In the main the criticism centered about the news service, the editorials and the general lack of integrity of the papers. There was no criticism of the newspapers for failure to know the facts; they were criticized rather for the failure to present an unbiased report. The same sort of criticism is made of the editorial columns. The editor is believed to be unduly influenced by the business manager. The phrase, "the potent censorship of Big Business," or some analogous expression, occurred so often that it seemed to express a general lack of confidence.

The present research was not devised to ascertain the degree of confidence in newspapers, and one would not be justified in asserting that the lack of confidence is general unless other grounds for the statement were at hand.

The newspaper that would be preferred by the representative business and professional men might not be popular with other classes of society.

The Ideal Newspaper.

Judging from the answers of 2,000 men the conviction is forced upon one that they do not care to have a newspaper serve as interpreter, defender or advocate of the truth. All that is desired is a brief but comprehensive publication of the news. That editor will be the most appreciated who selects the news most wisely and presents the unvarnished truth in all matters in which the constituency are interested. Some persons have no interest in the sporting pages; others never admit reading crimes and casualties. Individual interests are so varied that no paper can expect general circulation without criticism from many readers because of the events emphasized in news gathering. However, the readers do not complain generally because of the presence of pages of material that they never read. The man who is not interested in finance, sports, etc., does not complain because of the presence of these things. He does complain because in place of a short and accurate account of things interesting to him, he finds long and inaccurate accounts of them. The ideal paper would have to do only with facts. The news would have to be well written, but the interest would be mainly in the news itself and not in the reporter's or the publisher's views concerning it.

There are many persons who read neither books nor monthly and weekly magazines. For them the daily newspaper must supply the place of all these. The storiette is their only literature. The editor and the reporter must interpret the daily events. The unbiased presentation of these daily events would not be adequate. For the business and professional man the circumstances are different. All of the 2,000 business and professional men answering my questionaire read much besides the daily papers. Their literary entertainment is found in books and magazines.

The whole reading world desires to secure pleasure from literature, to read articles which champion its rights and to follow some great leader in interpreting current events. That all these functions are performed in many instances by the daily press can not be doubted. That the better class of society has passed beyond this condition is likewise apparent. The results as presented above make it quite evident that for the vast majority the daily paper is merely a *news* paper. For this class the ideal paper would be the one that serves this interest most perfectly. Cartoons would find a place in such papers but they would not be the same sort of cartoons that appear in the monthly comic papers. Editorials would find a place but they would be in the main concise statements concerning important events. Special articles would be in place in such a paper but they would deal in the main with current events. The ideal daily would put its emphasis on the field that is not covered by the weeklies and monthlies. It would also present the events of the day in such form that they could be read in fifteen minutes; for the busy man does not devote more than that time to any daily paper.

The Newspaper as an Advertising Medium.

The question which the advertiser is sure to raise in this connection is, What sort of advertisements could be valuable in what might be an ideal paper for the so-called better classes? If the ideal paper is fully differentiated from the weeklies and monthlies in its "literary departments," has it not surrendered to them also the field of advertising except for the announcement of local sales and other similar events? Has it not ceased to be a competitor for national advertising? This conclusion does not follow; for the ideal newspaper, which had the full confidence of its readers, would be a powerful medium for all classes of advertisements. Success in advertising is based on confidence, and one reason why advertising rates are higher in weeklies and monthlies for a proportionate amount of circulation is the fact that at the present time people have more confidence in these than in the dailies.

Potential customers are not coldly logical and analytic in estimating commodities. An advertisement seen on garbage boxes may be a good advertisement and may announce real bargains but it possesses little influence. The same advertisement seen in a cherished household publication carries all the respect and trust that has been created by the other departments of the publication. We do not appreciate even good food if served upon dirty dishes. We are not influenced even by a good advertisement appearing in daily papers if they seem to us to be in any way unreliable.

The present research was not undertaken to discover the value of newspapers as advertising media for the better class of society, but to ascertain which motives would appeal most profoundly to this class of society in inducing them to subscribe for newspapers. Incidentally the fact is revealed that the newspapers do not have the confidence of many of this particular class of society. If later researches discover the fact that the lack of confidence is general with this class of society, the results may be disquieting to the publishers, but it will result in the production of some newspapers which conform to the demands of this great and influential body of citizens. The sensational newspaper may possess the confidence of the lower classes of society and hence be a good advertising medium for reaching that class. Unless the newspapers are a valuable medium with the better classes, they are not serviceable for many of the most influential advertisers. The hope for relief from sensational journalism is to be found only in the discovery of the fact that a very influential class of business and professional men cannot be influenced by advertisements appearing in sensational publications. That this hope will be realized may be confidently anticipated if we may judge from the similar results which have been brought about of recent years in our best weeklies and monthlies. A few years ago all these publications contained advertisements of patent medicines, questionable financial schemes, etc. Many readers were interested in these advertisements and the space was well paid for. The significant fact was discovered, however, that more advertising space could be sold in high grade magazines that did not accept such advertisements. The space in the cleaner publications was worth more simply because such publications secured the confidence of the class of society that had the money necessary to purchase the advertised goods.

The value of a publication as an advertising medium is in a large degree determined by the particular class of citizens whose confidence it possesses. This is shown in monthlies, weeklies and dailies. For instance, for every thousand of circulation the advertising space in the Century Magazine is worth 178 per cent. more than that in the Popular Magazine; and likewise, space in Collier's Weekly sells for 233 per cent. more than space in Hearst's Sunday Magazine. The Chicago evening papers are not able to secure so much for advertising space as the morning papers, circulation considered. The results of the investigation concerning the opinions of the 2,000 Chicago business and professional men show that the Chicago paper which was most often preferred in proportion to its total circulation is the paper that secures, in proportion to circulation, a larger price than any of the others for its advertising space. That paper which was the least often preferred is the one which is compelled to sell its advertising space the cheapest, circulation being considered in both particulars.

It will not be necessary for the better classes of society to boycott the firms advertising in the sensational newspapers — although such action might hasten the day of relief. If a large proportion of the better classes of society lack confidence in newspapers, then these publications are not so valuable as advertising media as they might be. Sooner or later the publishers will find out the facts. Newspapers are sure to conform to the demands of the people because any other policy would be suicidal on the part of the publishers. Probably from fifty to ninety per cent. of the total income from any newspaper is derived from its advertising pages. Anything which makes these pages valuable will be diligently sought for even though the policy adopted may reduce the total subscription list.

In all the answers received from business and professional men there was no expression of a hope that the newspapers would ever be better than at present. The sentiment seemed to be common that they were getting worse. Two facts, however, render this pessimistic conclusion at least uncertain if not improbable. The first fact is that the newspapers are primarily dependent for their life upon the income from their advertising. The second fact is that the value of these pages is largely determined by the confidence which the public has in the paper as a whole; for lack of confidence in one part is unconsciously extended to all parts. The better American metropolitan daily is a wonderful embodiment of enterprise. If it would be strengthened as an advertising medium by an increased confidence on the part of the better classes of society, it is quite certain that the publishers will be equal to the emergency and will produce a paper that meets the enlightened and cultured demands.

Conclusion.

The questionnaire method is available in securing data valuable in planning an advertising campaign. If the questions asked are reasonable and interesting and if the motives of the person carrying on the research are not questioned, a large proportion of business and professional men will fill out the blank.

Most business and professional men read more than one daily and hence may be reached by an advertisement even though it is not inserted in all the papers. Advertisements inserted both in the best and also in the poorer papers are largely lost in the latter because of duplication of circulation.

Most business and professional men spend about fifteen minutes daily reading papers. The amount of time spent in reading advertisements must be very small. Hence advertisements should be so constructed that they will carry their message at a single glance.

Business and professional men subscribe for dailies because of the desire for news. Prizes, editorials, storiettes, etc., are of secondary importance in inducing these men to subscribe for any particular paper.

These business and professional men lacked confidence in their preferred daily papers. Hence advertisements seen in such publications do not have the greatest possible influence. The newspaper is, from the publisher's point of view, primarily an advertising medium and can attain its maximum value only when it secures the full confidence of its readers. This fact may lead to an improvement in the ethical standards of our daily papers.

XVII
BIBLIOGRAPHY

The literature upon the subject of advertising is not as good as we might wish, but it is too important to be neglected by anyone interested in business promotion. The books and magazines cited in the following lists have been carefully selected, and although some of them are of relatively minor significance, a familiarity with them is well worth the while of all vitally concerned with the science or the art of advertising.

THE FOLLOWING IS A SELECTED LIST OF THE BEST BOOKS IN ENGLISH UPON THE SUBJECT OF ADVERTISING.

AMERICAN PRINTER.

THE AMERICAN MANUAL OF TYPOGRAPHY. *The Oswald Publishing Co., New York, 1905, pp. 105, $4.00.* An exhaustive exposition of the various phases of type-composition. This volume is prepared by a number of experts and represents the best in typography.

BAKER, WILLIAM H.

ADVERTISING PHRASES. *Chicago, 1901, pp. 50.* (Gist-of-Things-Library, vol. 3.)

BALMER, THOMAS.

SOME SUNKEN ROCKS IN ADVERTISING. *Butterick Co., New York, 1906, pp. 26.*

BATES, CHARLES AUSTIN.

THE ART AND LITERATURE OF BUSINESS. *Bates Advertising Co., New York, 1902, 6 volumes, pp. 2221, $25.00.* The work contains no table of contents and the index fills the entire sixth volume of 324 pages. The work is intended to be an encyclopedia of advertising although this is not made clear by the title. It is in the main a most creditable production and in spite of minor deficiencies should be a part of every advertiser's library.

BATES, CHARLES AUSTIN.

GOOD ADVERTISING. *Holmes Publishing Co., New York, 1896, pp. 599, $5.00.* The book contains over one hundred chapters and may almost be spoken of as an encyclopedia of advertising.

BIRD, THOMAS ALEXANDER.

SALES PLANS. *The Merchants' Record Co., Chicago, 1906, pp. 282, $2.50.* A book filled with schemes for increasing business. A collection of three hundred and thirty-three successful ways of getting business, including a great variety of practical plans that have been used by retail merchants to advertise and sell goods.

CALKINS, ERNEST ELMO AND HOLDEN, RALPH.

MODERN ADVERTISING. *D. Appleton & Co., New York, 1905, pp. 361, $1.50.* This is one of the best books on advertising and contains the following chapters: Definition of Advertising; History of Advertising; Channels of Trade; Magazines and Newspapers; Mural Advertising; The General Advertiser; The Advertising Manager; The General Advertising Agency; Retail Advertising; Mail-Order Advertising; The Mathematics of Advertising; Styles of Advertising; Some Mechanical Details.

CASTAREDE, L. DE.

MONEY-MAKING BY AD-WRITING. *Neuman and Castarede, London, 1905, pp. 367, 10s, 6d.* This book is intended for beginners in advertising and contains the following chapters: Composition and Style in Writing Advertisements; Technical Proof and Press Corrections; Block Type; Illustrations; Small Advertisements; Newspaper Advertising; Magazine Advertising; Circularising; Ratio of Advertising to Returns; Poster Advertising; How to "Key" Advertisements; The Psychology of Advertising; also several other chapters of less importance. The author makes much use of the American contributions to the literature of advertising. This is especially apparent in the chapter on The Psychology of Advertising which consists almost entirely of quotations from The Theory of Advertising, by Scott, though no mention of this fact is made by the author.

DeWeese, Trauman A.

THE PRINCIPLES OF PRACTICAL PUBLICITY. *The Matthews-Northrup Works, Buffalo, 1906, pp. 244.* A treatise on the art of advertising. Sold only as a part of Business Man's Library, System Co., Chicago. The following are the chapter titles: Modern Commercial Publicity; What is Advertising? Mediums Employed by General and Direct Publicity; What is Good Advertising Copy? The Bull's-eye Method in Advertising; "Reason-Why Copy;" The Magazine and the Newspaper; Relative Values of Magazine Pages; Mail-Order Advertising; Follow-up Systems; The Booklet in Mail-Order Advertising; "Keying" Mail-Order Advertisements; Bank Advertising; Street Car Advertising; Railway and Steamship Advertising; Outdoor Advertising; Planning an Advertising Campaign; The Advertising Agency. This is one of the best books on the subject of advertising.

Farrington, Frank.

RETAIL ADVERTISING FOR DRUGGISTS AND STATIONERS. *The Baker & Taylor Co., New York, 1901, pp. 244, $1.00.* Chatty, interesting and instructive. Contains the following chapters: Excuse; In a General Way; Newspaper Advertising; Circular Advertising; Window Display; Odds and Ends; Store Management; One Hundred Sample Ads.

Fowler, Nathaniel C.

ABOUT ADVERTISING AND PRINTING. *S. Barta & Co., Boston, 1889, pp. 160, $2.00.* This volume treats of the same general subjects as the author's encyclopedia. This later book is, however, more adequate and is the product of later years.

FOWLER, NATHANIEL C.

BUILDING BUSINESS. *The Trade Co., Boston, 1893, pp. 518, $4.50.* This book covers in part the material which is more adequately treated in the author's later volume. (below)

FOWLER, NATHANIEL C.

FOWLER'S PUBLICITY. *Publicity Publishing Co., Boston, 1889, Q. pp. 1016, $15.00.* An encyclopedia of advertising, printing and all that pertains to the Public-Seeing Side of Business. Out of print, to be had only at second hand. The most pretentious and complete work on advertising.

GALE, HARLOW.

ON THE PSYCHOLOGY OF ADVERTISING. *Published by the author, Minneapolis, Minn., 1900, pp. 32, $0.75.* The author of this pamphlet seems to have been the first to apply experimental methods to the subject.

HENDERSON, R.

HENDERSON'S SIGN PAINTER. *Published by the author, Newark, N. J., 1906, pp. 112, $3.00.* A compilation of the very best creations from the very best artists in their specialties, embracing all the standard alphabets; also all the modern and fashionable styles of the times. The book contains nothing more than the title indicates. The price is excessive.

INTERNATIONAL CORRESPONDENCE SCHOOLS.

RETAIL ADVERTISING. *International Textbook Co., Scranton, Penn., 1905, two volumes, each of over 400 pages, $4.00 per volume, but not to be had except in sets of 5 volumes.* The following are the chapter heads: Copy and Proof; Supplementary Advertising; Retail Advertising Management; Conducting an Advertising Office; Department Store Advertising; Advertisement Illustration; Advertisement Construction; Principles of Display; Illustrations in Newspaper Advertisements; Engraving Process; Advertisements for Various Businesses; Cyclopedia of Retail Advertisements and Selling Points; Printing-House Methods; Exhibit of

Advertising Types and Borders. Each chapter is written by an expert. Chapters are being added from time to time and the whole "course" bids fair to be the best encyclopedia of advertising.

INTERNATIONAL CORRESPONDENCE SCHOOL.
LETTERING AND SIGN PAINTING. *International Textbook Co., Scranton, Penn., 1902, pp. 237, $4.00, but to be had only in connection with 4 other volumes (as above).*

INTERNATIONAL CORRESPONDENCE SCHOOLS.
SHOW-CARD WRITING. *International Textbook Co., Scranton, Penn., 1903, pp. 172; in addition many pages of illustrations, $4.00, but to be had only in connection with four other volumes (as above).*

MACDONALD, J. ANGUS.
SUCCESSFUL ADVERTISING: HOW TO ACCOMPLISH IT. *The Lincoln Publishing Co., Philadelphia, 1902, pp. 400, $2.00.* The book contains the following five chapters: Advertisement Building; Retail Advertising all the Year Around; Special Features in Retail Advertising; Mail Order Advertising; Miscellaneous Advertising. The book contains much advice, numerous illustrations of good ways of saying things, and is altogether a helpful book for the beginner in advertising.

MACGREGOR, T. D.
PUSHING YOUR BUSINESS. *Bankers' Publishing Co., New York, 1907, pp. 22, $1.00.* Devoted primarily to financial and real estate advertising.

MAHIN, JOHN LEE.
LECTURES ON ADVERTISING. *Mahin Advertising Co., Chicago, 1907, pp. 76, $1.00.*

MAHIN, JOHN LEE.
MAHIN'S ADVERTISING DATA BOOK. *Mahin Advertising Co., Chicago, 1908, pp. 556, $2.00.*

MORAN, CLARENCE.

THE BUSINESS OF ADVERTISING. *Methuen & Co., London, 1905. pp. 191, 2s, 6d net.* The book contains the following chapters: Advertising and Its Utility; History of Advertising; Manual of Advertising; Advertising in the Press; Advertising by Circular; The Pictorial Poster (other chapters and appendices are purely local in interest).

MORISON, FRANCIS R.

BANKING PUBLICITY. *Moody Publishing Co., New York, 1904, pp. 162, $4.00.* A manual on the art of advertising the business of financial institutions, containing numerous practical illustrations of appropriate wording and typographical arrangement of financial advertisements and forms of "follow-up" letters.

PAGE, EDWARD T.

ADVERTISING. *The Publicity Publishing Co., Chicago, 1903, pp. 255, $2.50.* How to plan, prepare, write and manage advertising; a course in the practical application of successful advertising.

POWELL, GEORGE HENRY.

POWELL'S PRACTICAL ADVERTISER. *G. H. Powell, New York, 1905, pp. 229, $5.00.* A practical work for advertisement writers and business men, with instructions on planning, preparing, placing and managing modern publicity. With cyclopedia of over one thousand useful advertisements.

PUBLISHERS' ADVERTISING BUREAU.

RETAIL AD. WRITING SIMPLIFIED. *Publishers' Advertising Bureau, Galesburg, Ill., pp. 108, $1.50.* A simple and comprehensive course of instruction for the preparation of successful advertising. The price is excessive. The author (or authors) appears to be a youth who has infinite faith in his own ideas.

RICE, A. E.

PRACTICAL BANK ADVERTISING. *Fremont Publishing Co., Fremont, Ohio, 1900, pp. 745, $10.00.* A cyclopedia of advertising information for financial institutions.

ROGERS, W. S.

A BOOK OF THE POSTER. *Greening & Co., London, 1901, pp. 158, 7s, 6d.* Illustrated with examples of the work of the principal poster artists of the world.

ROWELL, GEORGE PRESBURY.

FORTY YEARS AN ADVERTISING AGENT, *1865–1905. Printers' Ink Publishing Co., New York, 1906, 517 pp., $2.00.* The book contains no table of contents but is subdivided into fifty-two "papers;" the contents of the book are mainly reminiscence but the style of the author is so pleasing that the papers will be found interesting even by those who have never known the author personally.

SAMPSON, HENRY.

A HISTORY OF ADVERTISING FROM THE EARLIEST TIMES. *Chatto & Windus, London, 1874, pp. 616, 7s, 6d.* Illustrated by anecdotes, curious specimens and biographical notes. The book is exactly what the title asserts and has supplied many an interesting story or illustration for speakers before advertising clubs.

SAWYER, SAMUEL.

SECRETS OF THE MAIL-ORDER TRADE. *Sawyer Publishing Co., New York, 1900, pp. 180, $1.00.* The book is confined to the subject named in the title and is rather well written and instructive.

SCOTT, WALTER DILL.

THEORY OF ADVERTISING. *Small, Maynard & Co., Boston, 1903, pp. 240, $2.00, net.* A Simple Exposition of the Principles of Psychology in Their Relation to Advertising. This book is the first volume in which psychological principles are thus applied, and hence the book may be said to have created a new era in the science of advertising. The book contains the following chapters: The Theory of Advertising; Attention; Association of Ideas; Suggestion; The Direct Command; The Psychological Value of the Return Coupon; Psychological Experiment; Perception; Illusions of Perception; Illusions of Apperception; Personal Differences in Mental Imagery; Practical Application of Mental Imagery; Conclusion.

SMITH, WILLIAM.

ADVERTISE. HOW? WHEN? WHERE? *Routlege, Warne & Routlege, London, 1863, 1s.* The book lacks the modern practical point of view.

STEAD, WILLIAM.

THE ART OF ADVERTISING. *T. B. Browne, London, 1899, pp. 151, 3s, 6d.* This is one of the better foreign books but is not up to the American standard.

STRONG, CHARLES JAY.

THE ART OF SHOW CARD WRITING. *The Detroit School of Lettering, Detroit, 1907, pp. 209, $2.50.* A modern treatise on show card writing, designed as an educator in all branches of the art, with two hundred fifty-six illustrations and thirty lettering plates, comprising all the standard ancient and modern styles.

THOMPSON, J. WALTER.

THE THOMPSON BLUE BOOK ON ADVERTISING. *J. Walter Thompson & Co., New York, Chicago and Boston, 1906, pp. 238.* A Register of Representative Organs and How to Use Them. The book is in the main a register of newspapers and other publications with a statement of the supposed circulation of each and the advertising rate. The book is published in the interest of an advertising agency and presents numerous illustrations of the work of the agency. Incidentally much information concerning advertising is presented.

THOMPSON, W. A.

MODERN SHOW CARD LETTERING DESIGNS AND ADVERTISING PHRASES. *W. A. Thompson, Pontiac, Mich., 1906, pp. 112, $1.00.* A practical treatise on up-to-date pen and brush lettering, giving instruction respecting many styles of alphabets, shading, spacing, figuring and show card designing.

TRACY, CHARLES A.
THE ART OF DECORATING SHOW WINDOWS AND INTERIORS. *The Merchants' Record Co., Chicago, 1906, pp. 410, $3.50.* "A complete manual of window trimming designed as an educator in all the details of the art, according to the best accepted methods and treating fully every important subject."

WAGONSELLER, G. W.
THEORY AND PRACTICE OF ADVERTISING. *Wagonseller Publishing House, Middlebury, Pa., 1903, pp. 64, $1.00.*

THE FOLLOWING IS A LIST OF THE BOOKS ON PSYCHOLOGY WHICH ARE MOST HELPFUL TO BUSINESS MEN.

ANGELL, JAMES R.
PSYCHOLOGY. *Henry Holt & Co., New York, 1908, pp. 410. $1.50.* Modern, scientific and practical.

BALDWIN, JAMES MARK.
THE STORY OF THE MIND. *D. Appleton & Co., New York, 1901, pp. 232, small, $0.35.* An excellent little book and is found by business men to be of interest and value.

BETTS, GEORGE HERBERT.
THE MIND AND ITS EDUCATION. *D. Appleton & Co., New York, 1906, pp. 265, $1.25.*

HALLECK, REUBEN POST.
EDUCATION OF THE CENTRAL NERVOUS SYSTEM. *Macmillan Co., New York, 1904, $1.00.*

HALLECK, REUBEN POST.
PSYCHOLOGY AND PSYCHIC CULTURE. *American Book Co., New York, 1895, pp. 368, $1.25.*

HOFFMAN, FRANK SARGENT.
PSYCHOLOGY AND COMMON LIFE. *G. P. Putnam's Sons, New York, 1903, pp. 286, $1.30.*

JAMES, WILLIAM.

PSYCHOLOGY, BRIEFER COURSE. *Henry Holt & Co., New York, 1900, pp. 478, $1.60.* This is in many ways the most significant volume that has yet been written in English on psychology. The general reader may begin his reading of the book at page 134, as the first 133 pages involve a knowledge of physiology.

JAMES, WILLIAM.

TALKS TO TEACHERS ON PSYCHOLOGY. *Henry Holt & Co., New York, 1901, pp. 301, $1.50.* Although this book was written primarily for teachers, it will be found valuable to business men.

JASTROW, JOSEPH.

THE SUBCONSCIOUS. *Houghton, Mifflin & Co., Boston, 1905. pp. 549, $2.50.* The best book on the phase of psychology indicated by the title.

MÜNSTERBERG, HUGO.

PSYCHOLOGY AND LIFE. *Houghton, Mifflin & Co., Boston, 1899, pp. 286, $2.50.*

SCOTT, WALTER DILL.

THE PSYCHOLOGY OF PUBLIC SPEAKING. *Pearson Brothers, Philadelphia, 1907, pp. 222, $1.25.*

SCOTT, WALTER DILL.

THEORY OF ADVERTISING. *Small, Maynard & Co., Boston, 1903, pp. 240, $2.00 net.* A Simple Exposition of the Principles of Psychology in Their Relation to Advertising.

SCRIPTURE, E. W.

THE NEW PSYCHOLOGY. *Charles Scribner's Sons, New York, 1898, pp. 500, $1.25.*

SCRIPTURE, E. W.

THINKING, FEELING AND DOING. *G. P. Putnam's Sons, New York, 1907, pp. 266, $1.75.*

BIBLIOGRAPHY

SIDIS, BORIS.

THE PSYCHOLOGY OF SUGGESTION. *D. Appleton & Co., New York, 1898, pp. 386, $1.75.*

STRATTON, GEORGE MALCOM.

EXPERIMENTAL PSYCHOLOGY AND ITS BEARING UPON CULTURE. *Macmillan Co., New York, 1903, pp. 331, $2.00.*

THORNDIKE, EDWARD LEE.

THE HUMAN NATURE CLUB. *Longmans, Green & Co., New York, 1902, pp. 235, $1.25.* The readers of this elementary work would doubtless desire some of the author's more advanced works after the completion of this introductory one.

TITCHENER, E. B.

OUTLINES OF PSYCHOLOGY. *Macmillan Co., New York, In Press, $1.50.*

TITCHENER.

A PRIMER OF PSYCHOLOGY. *Macmillan Co., New York, 1899, pp. 316, $1.00.*

WITMER, LIGHTMER.

ANALYTICAL PSYCHOLOGY. *Ginn & Co., New York, 1902, pp. 251, $1.50.*

WUNDT, WILHELM.

OUTLINES OF PSYCHOLOGY. *G. E. Stechert & Co., New York, 1902, pp. 342, $2.00.*

WUNDT, WILHELM.

HUMAN AND ANIMAL PSYCHOLOGY. *Macmillan Co., New York, 1894, pp. 454, $2.60.*

THE FOLLOWING MAGAZINES ARE DEVOTED TO THE SUBJECT OF ADVERTISING:

Adsense, Chicago, monthly.
Advertising, Chicago, monthly.
Advertising Agent, New York, monthly.

Advertising World, Columbus, O., monthly.
Agricultural Advertiser, Chicago, monthly.
Brains for the Retailer and Advertiser, Deposit, N. Y., weekly.
Circulating Manager, Chicago, monthly.
Fame, New York, monthly.
Fourth Estate, New York, weekly.
Judicious Advertising, Chicago, monthly.
Mail Order Journal, Chicago, monthly.
Mertz's Magazines, Los Angeles, Cal., monthly.
National Advertiser, New York, weekly.
Newspaperdom, New York, semi-monthly.
Practical Advertising, Atlanta, Ga., monthly.
Profitable Advertising, Boston, monthly.
Printers' Ink, New York, weekly.
Publicite, Montreal, Quebec, Can., monthly.
Signs of the Times, Cincinnati, monthly.
Street Railway Advertising Quarterly, New York, quarterly.
Western Monthly, Kansas City, monthly.
White's Class Advertising, Chicago, monthly.
White's Sayings, Washington, monthly.

THE FOLLOWING IS A LIST OF THE BEST ARTICLES ON THE SUBJECT OF ADVERTISING FOUND IN MAGAZINES OTHER THAN THOSE DEVOTED EXCLUSIVELY TO ADVERTISING.

ALGER, G. W.

UNPUNISHED COMMERCIAL CRIME. *Atlantic Monthly, Vol. 94: 170–178, August, 1904.*

ATLANTIC MONTHLY.

SWINDLING AND NEWSPAPER ADVERTISING. *Vol. 94: 284–286, August, 1904.*

BAXTER, SYLVESTER.

THE NUISANCE OF ADVERTISING. *Century, Vol. 73: 419–430, January, 1907.*

BIBLIOGRAPHY

BELCHER, JOSEPH J.
NEWSPAPER ADVERTISEMENTS. *Harper's Magazine, Vol. 33: 781–789, November, 1866.*

BRADY, CYRUS TOWNSEND.
MAGAZINE CIRCULATION AND ADVERTISING. *The Critic, Vol. 47: 168–171, August, 1905.*

BROWN, WALTER BARRETT.
BOOK ADVERTISING FROM THE INSIDE. *Gunther's Magazine Vol. 26: 435–440, May, 1904.*

BRUSH, GEORGE SABIN.
STREET RAILWAY ADVERTISING. *Street Railway Journal, Vol. 28: 331–333, Sept. 1, 1906.*

CHAPIN, CHARLES H. B.
ELECTRIC CENTRAL STATION ADVERTISING. *Cossier's Magazine, Vol. 29: 461–465, April, 1906.*

CHOLMONDELEY, MARY.
AN ART IN ITS INFANCY. *The Monthly Review, Vol. 3: 79–90, June, 1901.*

CHRISTIAN, EDMUND B. V.
THE ADVERTISER'S SHAKESPEARE. *Gentlemen's Magazine, Vol. 271: 305–311, March, 1893.*

COLFORD, JULIAN KING.
THE SIGNS OF OLD LONDON. *St. Nicholas, Vol. 31: 160–166, 203–210, December, 1903, January, 1904.*

COLLINS, JAS. H.
THE ADVERTISEMENT WRITER. *The World To-day, Vol. 13: 1104–1108, November, 1907.*

COLLINS, JAS. H.
NOTES FOR A HISTORY OF BOOK PUFFERY. *Bookman, Vol. 24: 62–68, September, 1906.*

DAY, LEWIS F.
ART IN ADVERTISING. *Art Journal, Vol. 59: 49–, 1897.*

DELINEATOR.
THE SUBSTITUTION EVIL. *Delineator, Vol. 68: 697, November, 1906.* The Honor that is back of Advertising; Why Continued Advertising Pays.

DEWESSE, TRAUMAN A.
THE YOUNG MAN WITH NOTHING BUT BRAINS. *Forum, Vol. 32: 695–699, February, 1902.*

DIAL, THE.
BOOKS AND SHOES. *Vol. 5: 365–366, Dec. 1, 1905.*

ELLIS, G. STANLEY.
AGONY ADVERTISEMENTS. *Good Words, Vol. 41: 827–830, December, 1900.*

EVANS, RICHARDSON.
ADVERTISEMENT DISFIGUREMENT. *Westminster Review, Vol. 151: 244–258, March, 1899.*

EVANS, RICHARDSON.
ADVERTISING AS A TRESPASS ON THE PUBLIC. *The Nineteenth Century, Vol. 37: 968–980, June, 1895.*

EVANS, RICHARDSON.
ARCHITECTURE AND ADVERTISING. *Journal of the Society of Arts, Vol. 42: 35–44, Dec. 19, 1893.*

FORBES, W. D.
A QUESTION OF GOOD ADVERTISING. *Cossier's Magazine, Vol. 29: 515–518, April, 1906.*

FOWLER, NATHANIEL, C.
ADVERTISING, PAST, PRESENT, FUTURE. *The Arena, Vol. 29: 638–643, June, 1903.*

BIBLIOGRAPHY

FRENCH, GEORGE.
THE PRINCIPLES OF BOOK ADVERTISING. *The Dial, Vol. 40: 5–6, Jan. 1, 1906.*

FRISH, W. P.
ARTISTIC ADVERTISING. *Magazine of Art, Vol. 12: 421–427, 1889.*

HAINES, C. W.
DEFACING PROPERTY. *Nation, Vol. 85: 76, July 25, 1907.*

HARPER'S WEEKLY.
HOW TO CURB BILL-POSTERS. *Vol. 51: 1020, July 13, 1907.*

HARRIS, EMERSON P.
THE ECONOMIES OF ADVERTISING. *Social Economies, Vol. 4: 171–174, March, 1893.*

HARVEY, GEORGE.
OF HONESTY IN ADVERTISING. *North American Review, Vol. 183: 693–695, Oct. 5, 1906.*

HARTT, ROLLIN LYNDE.
THE HUMORS OF ADVERTISING. *Atlantic Monthly, Vol. 93: 602–612, May, 1904.*

HAYWARD, A.
THE ADVERTISING SYSTEM. *Edinburgh Review, Vol. 77: 1–43, February, 1843.*

HEINRICHS, ERNEST H.
THE ART OF SUCCESSFUL ADVERTISING. *Engineering Magazine, Vol. 6: 229–233, November, 1893.*

HERZEBERG, OSCAR.
THE EVOLUTION OF NEWSPAPER ADVERTISING. *Lippincott's Magazine, Vol. 60: 107–112, July, 1897.*

HOUSTON, HERBERT S.
BRITISH AND AMERICAN ADVERTISING. *World's Work (London), Vol. 2: 401–403, September, 1903.*

INDEPENDENT.

A THEATRICAL PRESS AGENT'S CONFESSION AND APOLOGY. *Vol. 59: 191–196, July 27, 1905.*

ADVERTISING THE GOSPEL. *Vol. 58: 196–201, Jan. 26, 1905.*

JENKINS, MACGREGOR.

HUMAN NATURE AND ADVERTISING. *Atlantic Monthly, Vol. 94: 393–401, September, 1904.*

KEMP, R. W.

ETHICS OF ADVERTISING. *The Bookman, Vol. 25: 31–32, March, 1907.*

KIMBALL, ARTHUR REED.

BINDING ADVERTISEMENTS IN SERIALS. *The Library Journal, Vol. 28: 766–767, November, 1903.*

KIMBALL, ARTHUR REED.

THE FIGHT AGAINST ADVERTISING DISFIGUREMENT. *Scribner's Magazine, Vol. 29: 101–105, January, 1901.*

KIMBALL, ARTHUR REED.

THE MODERN HIGHWAY. *Independent, Vol. 52: 307–310, Feb. 1, 1900.*

LANG, ANDREW.

LITERATURE AND ADVERTISEMENT. *Independent, Vol. 55: 2088–2090, Sept. 3, 1893.*

LOGAN, J. D.

SOCIAL EVOLUTION AND ADVERTISING. *Canadian Magazine, Vol. 28: 330–334, February, 1907.*

LOW, WILL H.

THE RIGHT TO KEEP THE WORLD BEAUTIFUL. *Scribner's Magazine, Vol. 34: 507–512, October, 1903.*

MACDONAGH, MICHAEL.
THE CRAFT OF NEWSPAPER ADVERTISING. *Monthly Review, Vol. 20: 102–113, August, 1905.*

MALTBIE, MILO ROY.
ADVERTISING SIGNS AND ART. *Municipal Affairs, Vol. 5: 738–753, September, 1901.*

MATAJA, VICTOR.
THE ECONOMIC VALUE OF ADVERTISING. *International Quarterly, Vol. 8: 379–398, December, 1903.* (A forceful presentation of the possible evils of advertising.)

MCDOUGAL, WILLIAM H.
THE ADVERTISING PAGE. *Overland Monthly, Vol. 22: 569–572, December, 1893.*

MEYER, ANNIE NATHAN.
AMONG THE FEBRUARY MAGAZINES. *The Bookman, Vol. 17: 20–22, March, 1903.*

MUNICIPAL AFFAIRS.
MUNICIPAL ÆSTHETICS FROM A LEGAL STANDPIONT. *Vol. 3: 715–723, December, 1899.*

NATION.
FINANCIAL ADVERTISEMENTS. *Vol. 9: 186–187, Sept. 2, 1869.*
ART AND ADVERTISING. *Vol. 20: 342–343, May 20, 1875.*
MUNICIPAL ADVERTISING. *Vol. 66: 240, March 13, 1898.*
EVERY AUTHOR HIS OWN PRESS AGENT. *Vol. 73: 86–87, Aug. 1, 1901.*
POSTER REGULATIONS. *Vol. 74: 146–147, Feb. 20, 1902.*
REGULATION OF PUBLIC ADVERTISING. *Vol. 78: 163–164, March 3, 1904.*

NEW REVIEW.
THE ADVERTISING NUISANCE. *Vol. 9: 466–481, November, 1893.* (Discussed by W. E. H. Seeky, Walter Besant, Mary Jeune, W. B. Richmond and Julian Sturges.)

OMSTED, FREDERICK LOW.
REFORM IN PUBLIC ADVERTISING. *Brush and Pencil, Vol. 6: 247–256, September, 1900.*

ONCE A WEEK.
THE PHILOSOPHY OF ADVERTISING. *Vol. 9: 163–165, August, 1863.*

OUTLOOK.
TAXING SIGNS. *Vol. 78: 657–659, November 12, 1904.*

POWERS, JOHN O.
ADVERTISING. *Annals of American Academy of Political and Social Science, Vol. 22: 470–474, November, 1903.*

QUARTERLY REVIEW.
ADVERTISEMENTS. *Vol. 97: 183–225, May, 1855.*

RANDELL, WILFRID L.
THE POSTER AND THE PUBLIC. *Living Age, Vol. 36: 509–511, Aug. 24, 1907.*

REID, ANDREW.
HISTORY IN ADVERTISING. *Fortnightly Review, Vol. 72: 576–588, October, 1899.*

REPPLIER, AGNES.
"AS ADVERTISED." *Lippincott's Magazine, Vol. 66: 912–917, December, 1900.*

REVIEW OF REVIEWS (American).
ADVERTISING IN FRANCE. *Vol. 23: 485–486, April, 1901.*
THE PLACE OF ADVERTISING IN MODERN BUSINESS. *Vol. 23: 612–614, May, 1901.*
THE GROWTH OF ADVERTISING. *Vol. 29: 101–102. January, 1904.*

ROBINSON, C. M.
ABUSES OF PUBLIC ADVERTISING. *Atlantic Monthly, Vol. 93: 289–299, March, 1904.*

BIBLIOGRAPHY

ROBINSON, C. M.

ARTISTIC POSSIBILITIES OF ADVERTISING. *Atlantic Monthly, Vol. 94: 53–60, July, 1904.*

SCIENTIFIC AMERICAN, SUPPLEMENT.

AUTOMATIC, CHANGEABLE ELECTRIC SIGNS. *Vol. 51, 21087–21088, March 23, 1901.*

SCOTT, W. D.

PSYCHOLOGY OF ADVERTISING. *Atlantic Monthly, Vol. 93: 29–36, January, 1904.*

SCRIBNER'S MAGAZINE.

A PLEA FOR BETTER STREET CAR POETRY. *Vol. 31: 378–380, March, 1902.*

ON THE OWNERSHIP OF YOURSELF. *Vol. 34: 633–634, November, 1903.*

SHEAFER, HENRY C.

A STUDY IN ADVERTISING. *The Arena, Vol. 29: 384–390, April, 1903.*

SEEDS, RUSSEL M.

ORGANIZING THE MACHINE-SELLING DEPARTMENT. *Engineering Magazine, Vol. 27: 762–767, August, 1904.*

SHERMAN, SIDNEY A.

ADVERTISING IN THE UNITED STATES. *American Statistical Association, New Series No. 52: 1–44, December, 1900.* (This is one of the most scientific articles that has yet appeared on the subject of advertising.)

SHORE, W. TEIGEMOUTH.

THE CRAFT OF THE ADVERTISER. *Fortnightly Review, Vol. 81: 301–310, February, 1907.*

STUART, ESME.

ONLY THE ADVERTISEMENT. *Temple Bar, Vol. 106: 220–230, October, 1905.*

SWINTON, JOHN.
NEWSPAPER NOTORIETY. *Independent, Vol. 53: 211–213, Jan. 24, 1901.*

VAN NORMAN, LOUIS E.
ADVERTISING IDEAS. *Chautauquan, Vol. 39: 175–179, April, 1904.*

WAKEMAN, GEORGE.
ADVERTISING. *The Galaxy, Vol. 3: 202–211, January, 1867.*

WALDRON, GEORGE B.
WHAT AMERICA SPENDS IN ADVERTISING. *Chautauquan, Vol. 38: 155–159, October, 1903.*

WARNER, JOHN DEWITT.
ADVERTISING RUN MAD. *Municipal Affairs, Vol. 4: 269–293, June, 1900.*

WARNER, JOHN DEWITT.
ADVERTISING AND ADVERTISERS. *Municipal Affairs, Vol. 4: 772–774, December, 1900.*

WIGHT, PETER B.
THE REAL BILL-BOARD QUESTION. *Chautauquan, Vol. 37: 491–494, August, 1903.*

WILLIAMS, HENRY MATTHEWS.
THE STORY OF AN "AD." *The Arena, Vol. 19: 684–685, May, 1898.*

WILLIAMS, J. B.
THE EARLY HISTORY OF LONDON ADVERTISING. *Nineteenth Century, Number 369: 793–800, November, 1907.*

WISBY, HROLF.
MODERN ADVERTISING METHODS. *The Independent, Vol. 56: 260–264, Feb. 4, 1904.*

WOODRUFF, CLINTON ROGERS.
THE CRUSADE AGAINST BILLBOARDS. *Review of Reviews, Vol. 36: 345–349, September, 1907.*

YALE REVIEW.
THE PHILOSOPHY OF MODERN ADVERTISING. *Vol. 8: 229–232, November, 1899.*

A SUPPLEMENTARY LIST OF BOOKS ON ADVERTISING, PUBLISHED 1908–1910.

BALMER, EDWIN.
THE SCIENCE OF ADVERTISING. *Originally published by the author, Chicago, Ill., 1909; for sale by Duffield & Company, New York, 50 cents net.*

BARSODI, WILLIAM.
FINANCIAL ADVERTISING. *Barsodi Advertising Service, New York, 1909, pp. 128, $2.00.*

BELLAMY, FRANCIS, EDITOR.
EFFECTIVE MAGAZINE ADVERTISING. *With an introduction, "The Science of Advertising Copy," Mitchell Kennerley, New York, 1909, pp. 361, $5.00 net.*

BERKWITZ, WILLIAM LEONARD.
THE ENCYCLOPEDIA OF THE MAIL ORDER BUSINESS. *Published by the author, New York, 1908, pp. 270, $5.00.*

BUNTING, HENRY S.
SPECIALTY ADVERTISING. *Novelty News Press, Chicago, 1910, pp. 163.*

CHAPMEN, CLOWRY.
THE LAW OF ADVERTISING AND SALES. *Published by the author, Denver, 1908, two volumes, $10.00.*

COLLINS, JAMES H.
HUMAN NATURE IN SELLING GOODS. *Henry Altemus Co., Philadelphia, 1909, pp. 93, $0.50 net.*

CORBIN, WILLIAM A.
SALESMANSHIP DEPORTMENT AND SYSTEM. *G. W. Jacobs & Co., Philadelphia, 1907, pp. 380, $1.00.*

DELAND, LORIN F.
IMAGINATION IN BUSINESS. *Harper and Brothers, New York, 1909, pp. 108, $0.50.*

EDGAR, A. E.
HOW TO ADVERTISE A RETAIL STORE. *The Outing Press, Deposit, N. Y., 1908, pp. 504, $3.50.*

FOX, IRVING P. AND FORBES, B. A.
ONE THOUSAND WAYS AND SCHEMES TO ATTRACT TRADE. *Spatula Publishing Co., Boston, 1907, pp. 208, $1.00.*

FRENCH, GEORGE.
THE ART AND SCIENCE OF ADVERTISING. *Sherman, French & Co., Boston, 1909, pp. 291, $2.00 net.*

GULICK, LUTHER H.
MIND AND WORK. *Doubleday, Page & Co., New York, 1908, pp. 201, $1.20 net.*

HOLMAN, WASHINGTON C.
GINGER TALKS. *The Salesmanship Co., Chicago, 1908, pp. 206, $2.00.*

HOLMAN, WASHINGTON C.
TALKING POINTS AND SELLING ARGUMENTS. *Salesmanship Co., Chicago, 1908, pp. 516, $5.00.*

LENINGTON, NORMAN G.
SEVEN PRINCIPLES OF SUCCESSFUL ADVERTISING. *Commercial Science System, Scranton, Pa., 1908, pp. 141, $1.00.*

BIBLIOGRAPHY

LEWIS, E. ST. ELMO.
FINANCIAL ADVERTISING. *Levey Brothers & Co., Indianapolis, 1908, pp. 992, $5.00.*

LEWIS, HENRY HARRISON, AND DUFF, ORVA S.
HOW FORTUNES ARE MADE IN AVDERTISING. *Publicity Publishing Co., Chicago, 1908, pp. 242, $1.25.*

LEWIS, LAWRENCE.
THE ADVERTISEMENTS OF THE SPECTATOR. *Houghton, Mifflin Co., Boston, 1909, pp. 308, $2.00.*

LINDGREN, CHARLES.
THE NEW SALESMANSHIP AND HOW TO DO BUSINESS BY MAIL. *Laird & Lee, Chicago, 1909, pp. 190, $1.50.*

MACGREGOR, T. D.
PUSHING YOUR BUSINESS. *Bankers Publishing Co., New York, 1909, pp. 181, $1.00.*

PRATT, WILLIAM KNIGHT.
THE ADVERTISING MANUAL. *Daniel Stern, Chicago, 1909, pp. 278, $3.50.*

SYSTEM PUBLISHING CO.
HOW TO WRITE LETTERS THAT WIN. *System Publishing Co., Chicago, 1909, pp. 128.*

THAYER, JOHN ADAMS.
ASTIR. *Small, Maynard & Co., Boston, 1910, pp. 302, $1.20 net.*

WOOLLEY, EDWARD MOTT.
THE ART OF SELLING GOODS. *The American Business Man, Chicago, 1907, pp. 167.*